RED FIRE

GROWING UP DURING
THE CHINESE CULTURAL REVOLUTION

WEI YANG CHAO

Red Fire is an unforgettable historical testimony, plunging us into the most turbulent years of the Chinese Cultural Revolution. We travel alongside the young narrator and share his excitement, bewilderment, and rage, and by the end of the book we are forced to recognize that this is one of the greatest gifts literature can provide us: to recover a lost but living world.

—Jasmin Darznik, New York Times bestselling author of *The Good Daughter: A Memoir of My Mother's Hidden Life*

RED FIRE

GROWING UP DURING
THE CHINESE CULTURAL REVOLUTION

WEI YANG CHAO

AVANT PRESS

The stories in this book reflect the author's recollection of events. Some names, locations, and identifying characteristics have been changed to protect the privacy of those depicted. Dialogue has been recreated from memory.

RED FIRE Copyright © 2017 by Wei Yang Chao

For more information or to contact the author, visit WeiYangChao.com.

Edited by Jasmin Darznik
Book Cover and Interior Design: JM Shubin, Book Alchemist (bookalchemist.net)
Copy Editor: Bob Cooper (bob-cooper.com)
Author photograph: Yu Yuan

ISBN 978-0-9981960-1-5

First Printing in 2016
Published in the United States by Avant Press

I dedicate this book to my parents,
Bingquan Zhao and Jie Qin,
whose strength helped us endure the years
of the Cultural Revolution.

CONTENTS

Family photo taken in 1967 inside Beijing's Zizhuyuan Park, one year before the "Family Struggle Session."

The author, his older brother and younger sister at Beijing's Tian'anmen Square, holding copies of Chairman Mao's *Little Red Book*, taken at the start of the Cultural Revolution in 1966.

THE DAY THE REBELS CAME

Beijing, 1968

WE KNEW THE REBELS WOULD SHOW NO MERCY.

None of us had slept the night before. We'd been living with a sword hanging over our heads for weeks; that morning it seemed sure to fall. I was fifteen years old, the eldest son in the house now that my brother had been sent off to the countryside. These kinds of meetings were no longer strange to me. I'd already witnessed several struggle sessions first-hand. I knew that people were not only routinely humiliated but also tortured—sometimes they were almost beaten to death.

But while I was quite familiar with struggle sessions, this time the targets were my mother and father, and it was now my turn to betray those I loved.

My family had only recently moved from Guangdong, a province in the far south, thousands of miles away. In those days you lived and died in the same place you were born, but the government had transferred Father to Beijing a year earlier. His fluency in several languages, including English and Spanish, was a rare asset, but over the last few months he'd become a target at work.

I left the door open for the rebels, yet when they stormed our apartment they kicked it so hard I thought it would fly off the hinges. The apartment had been provided through Father's employer, the *Beijing Review*. It had two rooms, one for my parents and one for my sister and I. Including the kitchen and toilet, the floor space was just over 300 feet, but with the rebels stalking the rooms it felt positively tiny.

There were five or six of them, men and women in their twenties and thirties, along with two women from our local neighborhood committee. They didn't even bother to glance at us before setting up their props. One of the two plaques they'd brought with them read "Down with Anti-Revolutionary Zhao." Zhao was my father's name. The other plaque read: "Down with the Woman from a Landowner's Family." This one was presumably for my mother.

I held my breath, anxious not to betray the slightest emotion.

The rebels shouldered past me and marched into the bedroom my sister and I shared. I stood in the doorway, watching. Working together, they stood the two plaques against the wall, then rolled out a piece of red cloth with prominent white characters: *Meeting to Denounce Counter-Revolutionary Zhao.*

One of the rebels, a hulking man well over six feet tall,

jumped onto my bed and began nailing the banner to the wall.

"Take this outside!" he shouted, nodding at my sister's bed. "We need more room!"

How could I possibly manage to move the bed on my own? Father was still badly wounded from the last round of beatings; he couldn't lift anything heavy. I had no idea what to do, but then, without speaking, my mother and my younger sister picked up one end of the bed. I stepped forward and I picked up the other. When we reached the door, some kind-hearted neighbor lent us a hand. The others just watched as we tried to wrestle the bed out the front door.

I was stunned by their indifference. Until now we'd been on cordial terms with the two women from the neighborhood committee, but the expressions on their faces were now cold and cruel. *They must really think we're enemies of the state,* I thought to myself. I watched as some of the neighbors cheerfully waved in others. "Come on up!" they called to one another. It was as if a party was about to begin. One by one they filed into our apartment, all of them drawn not by sympathy but by curiosity or downright excitement.

I watched helplessly as two of the rebels shoved my father into the next room and slammed the door shut. A thin wall separated the apartment's two rooms. "Behave yourself and cooperate!" we heard the man shout, and then he began beating my father so hard that we could hear it from the other side of the wall. I winced at each blow and whimper.

Before long a large crowd had gathered in our apartment.

I recognized one of the people. It was Wang something or other, a Shanghai woman in her thirties who'd once worked as a translator at the *Beijing Review*. She was now the leader of the rebels, and she'd come to chair the struggle session. She had fair skin and an attractive figure, but her hawkish spectacles and sneer made her ugly to me.

"Come here!" she barked, snatching my mother's arm and leading her roughly from the room.

A few minutes later, when everything was finally in place, Wang shouted: "And now, the anti-revolutionary, Zhao!"

The door to the other room was thrown wide open. My heart skipped a beat as Father and Mother staggered into the room and were shoved onto the floor. Their heads were bent low and large plaques were hanging from their necks. Four rebels stepped up, pinning my parents' arms behind their backs.

I glanced at my younger sister. Her face was white as ash. She held my arm with all her might, but in that moment I couldn't comfort her. My mind was totally focused on my parents and how I could possibly save them.

My mother was shaking uncontrollably, her delicate, pretty face contorted in terror. As a young woman she'd studied piano in Fujian, where she became a music teacher. Until recently her life had been filled with music. As soon as a tune by Chopin, Mozart, or Beethoven drifted into the air, she lost herself in it. She existed through music.

But all that was over for her now. Western classical music had been banned. Mother had left her beloved piano back in Guangzhou, following my father to Beijing and working as a librarian. She never complained about her job, which was tedious; she loved Father too much to complain. Gentle and kind-hearted, she lacked the temperament to handle a situation like this, but as a landlord's daughter-in-law her fate was more or less sealed.

I wanted desperately to help her, but all I could do was to silently pray, *Be strong, Mother!*

Father was an even bigger worry. He seemed composed, but I knew he was faltering. He'd been accused of being a spy for the U.S. government—and that was just one of many accusations against him. He'd been dragged repeatedly to denunciation meetings; subjected again and again to interrogations and beatings; and forced to endure public humiliation time and again. Even after all of this, he still refused to accept the charges against him.

Father had attended college and graduate school in New York, that was true. But there was no way he was a spy— I knew it with every fiber of my being. Except for a few scientists who'd made outstanding contributions to the country, those who'd studied abroad were now labeled as spies working for either the U.S. or the Soviet Union.

My father was stubborn; it was for exactly this reason that he'd been tortured more viciously than others during the interrogations over the last several months. What, I wondered, would they do to him now?

I wouldn't have to wait long for the answer. That day they beat Father like an animal. Within minutes, he was slumped over, bleeding and seemingly unconscious. I tried to breathe, but my chest had seized up. I looked around the room. None of the neighbors said anything and there wasn't a trace of sympathy from the rebels' side. We were "class enemies," unworthy of even the slightest human decency.

It'll be over soon, I told myself over and over to calm myself. For weeks I'd been too worried to sleep at night. Ever since Father had been targeted the first time, I'd kept telling myself to be strong. But what if my parents couldn't endure what was happening? What if they committed suicide? Many people had done just that since the revolution began. I had to protect my parents, I kept saying to myself. The only way to keep them out of harm's way was to satisfy the rebels by holding a "successful" struggle session.

Nothing makes you grow up faster than pure misery. That day, life snapped in two. Soon it would splinter into bits. As China reeled and convulsed through the first bloody years of the Cultural Revolution, I would grow up very fast. But on that day in April 1968, I still thought that if I could just be strong I could save my family and myself.

I was wrong.

The author's father in New York Central Park in 1948.
A graduate of NYU, he returned to China determined to
contribute to the country's future.

A DANCE IN THE DARK

IN BEIJING, DURING THE CHINESE CULTURAL REVOLUTION, Mother and Father danced in the dark.

In the evenings, after closing the windows and drawing the curtains shut, Father would slide a record from its sleeve and place it gently onto the record player. Johann Strauss' "Blue Danube" and "Tales from the Vienna Woods" were his favorites. Sometimes my siblings and I watched our parents from the doorway as they danced. My sister Si Yan would cup her hands over her mouth, hiding her giggles, and my brother Xu Yang would rib me good-naturedly. Father would take Mother's hand and with that our small apartment turned into a private ballroom.

Western classical music was now forbidden, deemed a vestige of bourgeois society. Composers, conductors, musicians, and teachers were branded as "counter-revolutionaries" and sent away to re-education camps. Some were imprisoned and tortured; many died by their own hands. Just playing a waltz was a punishable offense.

Father kept the volume on the turntable turned to the lowest notch for fear that someone would overhear the music and report us to the local authorities. But even with music just barely audible and the lights turned off, Father and Mother danced beautifully. They swept from corner to corner, Father's hand delicately placed on the small of Mother's back and Mother quietly humming along to the waltz, both of them immersed in their dangerous, secret joy.

The revolution began in May 1966.

Mao Zedong, also known as Chairman Mao, inaugurated the huge political movement that would come to be known as the Chinese Cultural Revolution. Having grown up a peasant, he organized other Chinese peasants to eventually bring revolution to all of China, forcing his great rival Chiang Kai-shek to flee to Taiwan. Upon founding the People's Republic of China in 1949, Mao exulted, "The Chinese people, comprising one quarter of humanity, have stood up."

By the early 1960s Mao observed a troubling shift: party officials at all levels no longer seemed interested in pursuing revolutionary ideals. What's more, they had become privileged, bureaucratic, and alienated from the people. Mao now thought China might soon revert from socialism to capitalism.

He had every reason to worry.

It was two American brothers, John Foster Dulles and

Allen Dulles, who first advanced "peaceful evolution" as a strategy to combat Communism during the Cold War. John was Secretary of State and Allen was head of the CIA during this period. Allen Dulles was an interventionist, spearheading covert operations in Guatemala, Iran, and Cuba. Former U.S. President Richard Nixon once explained the Dulles' strategy in detail: "Peaceful evolution from socialism back to capitalism [aims] to surpass, penetrate, or get around the Iron Curtain. It is. . .a race between two social systems [that] will serve to speed up peaceful change in [China's] social system. . .breaking down Communism from the inside."

To Mao, the Soviet Union had already fallen victim to this so-called "peaceful evolution." There was no way he would allow China to follow suit, but he and the country's president, Liu Shaoqi, had very different ideas about the struggle ahead. Mao believed that to protect itself from the capitalist-imperialist West, China had to transform itself into a powerful nation-state. A permanent cultural revolution would be essential to that goal.

A battle of wills developed between Mao and Liu Shaoqi, and that battle came to a head in 1966.

That year Mao issued a searing indictment against the Party: "At every level in the Party's central committee, its departments, in provincial, municipal, and in autonomous regional levels, representatives of the capitalist class have found their way into our organizations. These representatives should be denounced and removed from their posts in our Party, the Government, and the People's Liberation Army. None of them should be trusted; none of them should be given charge of the leadership of this Cultural Revolution. Unfortunately, some of them—either in the past or present—are still there, and this is extremely dangerous."

Mao also took aim at President Liu Shaoqi. "The representatives of the capitalist class," he wrote in a document titled the *May Sixteenth Notice,* "have made their way into our Party, government, military, and cultural circles. They are anti-revolutionary revisionists, and if the situation allows, they will seize power, turning our proletariat dictatorship into a capitalist one. Some of them have now been seen through, but others haven't. With our trust, they are on their way to become the next generation of leaders. People like Nikita Khrushchev are lurking nearby, and Party committees on different levels must be on the alert!"

Even though his name wasn't mentioned overtly, everybody understood that "people like Nikita Khrushchev" referred to Liu Shaoqi. For the first time, the conflict between Mao and Liu Shaoqi had been made public.

The May Sixteenth Notice became the framework for the Cultural Revolution. Two months after its appearance, when Mao discovered that execution of the notice had been met with resistance, he was furious. Even more disconcerting to Mao, Liu Shaoqi's influence inside the Party seemed to have survived intact, and many high-level government officials still stood firmly on Liu Shaoqi's side. They were slow to follow Mao's instructions, or else they merely feigned support in public but opposed him in secret.

For the first time since coming to power, Mao's authority

seemed less than absolute. China was under one-party rule, and as the Communist Party's leader, Mao had held ultimate power. Beginning in 1959, however, he had retreated from the front line, leaving governance of the state and leadership of the party temporarily to Liu Shaoqi. In the seven years that ensued, many high-level officials rallied around Liu Shaoqi. By 1966, he had become powerful enough to challenge Mao's authority. For his part, Mao never genuinely feared a power struggle—but the situation had to be remedied.

Mao was both an experienced and supremely confident leader; the only question was how to solve this particular problem.

For now, however, Mao harnessed his rage and contemplated his next move.

From earliest childhood, I was taught to think that the West—America especially—was on the verge of extinction. America was dying. No, it was already dead, destroyed by greed and decadence.

On my way to my elementary school in Guangdong Province, I'd gaze up at the many posters decrying the hateful "Yankees." Near the front gates to my school there was an enormous poster of a man in a tall, striped hat sitting astride a fallen U-2 missile. "Who's that?" I asked Father one day. His face darkened. "John Kennedy, the American President," he said. To Chinese-speakers, "Kennedy" sounded like "biting" and "ground," and the poster showed the president with his mouth to the dirt.

All this could be very confusing at times. I knew that Father was a patriot, and an ardent one. When Japanese occupation ended in 1945 and Hong Kong fell under British rule, millions migrated there from Mainland China. After finishing graduate school in the U.S. in 1950, Father, however, chose to move to the mainland rather than continue working for my grandfather in Hong Kong. As a result, Father would never see his own father again, but so far as I knew he never regretted the decision.

But Father had lived in America for several years as a young man, and he'd traveled to Europe as well. Even as a child I saw that these foreign places still lived inside him. If his passion for the waltz and other works of Western classical music wasn't enough proof of this, his love of coffee offered another clue.

China had always been a tea-drinking country. My father, however, had developed a taste for coffee as a college student at New York University. When he came back to China after graduate school, the country was under a U.S. embargo. There wasn't a single place in the whole country that sold coffee. Father went without his favorite beverage for many months, but then, on a trip to Hainan Island, an island off the Chinese mainland, he happened on the extraordinary: a coffee plant. He came back home with a small sack of coffee beans tucked in among his luggage.

These beans were a treasure to him. He'd stand in the kitchen, hammering a few of them into a fine powder and then boiling that powder in a small pot. Once, when he caught me watching him as he prepared his coffee, he waved me forward and told me to take a sip. I did, only to find it bitter. I made a sour face. He took the cup back, thought for a moment, and then spooned in a tiny amount of sugar. Our ration cards only allowed for a few ounces' worth of Cuban sugar, so I knew this was a very special treat. I took another sip, then handed it quickly back. Even with the sugar, I didn't like the taste, but the aroma pleased me—and so did the look on Father's face whenever he brought the rim of his coffee cup to his mouth.

Literature was Father's true passion. His bookcase, which we called his "library," stood in the main room of the apartment. It was stacked with the plays of William Shakespeare and poems of Walt Whitman. Classical poetry from the Tang Dynasty also graced the shelves. At night he'd take his place in his old cane armchair and read for hours. I'd find him sitting under a small pool of light, his legs crossed and a book balanced on his lap. One night it might be *Leaves of Grass*, another night, *Dream of the Red Chamber*. What never changed was the quality of complete absorption with which he read his beloved books.

Our new apartment in Beijing was small and spare, decorated with the few good pieces of furniture we'd brought with us from Guangdong. Some of our things, like Father's armchair, were in the older Chinese style— fashioned from genuine wood and beautifully crafted. Others had followed Father from his travels abroad. There was a chest with a metal cover we called our "San Francisco-style cabinet." Father's bookshelf, also shipped from the States, had four shelves and was enclosed by glass. In the kitchen, a small fruit knife Father had brought back from

America took pride of place alongside the sturdy metal pots he'd also brought back from his travels.

Compared to the cheap, shabby furniture and trinkets we'd picked up in Beijing, these objects from the United States seemed incredibly durable. Like the music that filled Father and Mother's secret ballroom and the books that made up Father's library, we thought they would always be ours.

They wouldn't—but we had no idea yet how fragile these treasures were, nor what they would soon cost us.

Yi ku si tian. "Recall bitterness and reflect on sweetness."

Bitterness, I was taught to think when I was growing up, characterized China before the Revolution; our country's present was all sweetness. One very beautiful song from those years embodied this notion. Its lyrics went like this:

A starry evening sky,
A crescent moon hanging high.

At the meeting our production team held,
We aired our grievances and suffering of the old days.

In that vicious old society,
The poor shed such tears and blood, and bottled up their anger.

Each time I think of those years,
Tears stream down my face.

Set to a lovely tune, this song was very popular at the time. We sang it at every gathering to *yi ku si tian*—contrasting the misery of the past with today's happiness. And there were many such gatherings in those years.

Memories of famine were still vivid to most Chinese in the mid-sixties. In 1958 Mao had engineered a series of agricultural reforms that exacerbated food shortages and led to mass starvation. The Great Famine of 1958-1962 ended many millions of lives. I could still remember crowds of migrants standing outside the city in Guangdong. Hallow-cheeked and reed-thin, these Northerners had been drawn by rumors of the fertile Pearl River Delta, trekking south by the thousands to beg for food.

While I'd never experienced that kind of searing hunger, I would always remember the day when our extended family convened at my grandfather's home in Guangzhou to share a single bok choy. The house had three stories, with an inner courtyard and spacious rooms, space enough to house three families, my grandfather's, my father's and my uncle's. One day we all gathered on the rooftop to admire the lone bok choy that my mother had managed to grow in a clay pot. Once we'd all had a good long look at the precious vegetable, it was sliced into thin slivers so that everyone could savor a tiny piece.

I had a wicked sweet tooth as a boy, but I was rarely able to indulge it as cakes and candies were even less common than fruits and vegetables. One year at the Mid-Autumn Festival, Mother managed to buy a traditional mooncake with her food rations. The cakes consisted of a thin, tender pastry skin and sweet, dense filling, and the characters for "longevity" or "harmony;" images of flowers, vines, and rabbits graced the top. When Mother cut me a piece of the cake, I thrust the whole thing into my mouth, only to be disappointed. Hard and stale, that year's mooncake tasted of nothing so much as hunger.

When we moved to Beijing, I discovered other unpleasant tastes and encountered different hungers.

An important *yi ku si tian* ritual was to partake in a measly and revolting meal; this was meant to recall the hunger of years past. One day at my new school each of us was given a hunk torn from a steamed bun. It wasn't a proper bun made with wheat flour, but rather a mix of chaff and wild herbs. As someone from the south, I had never seen such a thing before—it was very coarse, very bitter, and very difficult to swallow. When I looked around, I saw that my schoolmates were just as put off by the bun as I was.

A popular saying drifted into my thoughts: "Miserable? Think of the Red Army's Long March. Exhausted? Think of the older generation who carried out the revolution." I always felt uneasy whenever my mother's landlord family background came up. Here, suddenly, was an opportunity to atone for her status.

I chewed this piece of so-called bread for a long time, but even so I barely managed to force it down my throat. Its purpose was well served, however—for after taking it, my guilt over my family background eased, my hatred for the old society increased, and my gratitude for the revolution grew strong.

✯✯✯

"Anything Mao says is ultimate truth," asserted Mao's successor, Lin Biao. "One of his words is equivalent to thousands of ours."

In the educational system of those years, Mao, Chairman of the Party, was afforded a godlike status. Lin Biao pushed the personality cult to the extreme even before the Cultural Revolution. It was Lin Biao who made the decision to gather Chairman Mao's sayings and print them in mass quantities. The result was the *Little Red Book*. More than a billion copies would eventually be published, making the diminutive book, wrapped in its distinctive red vinyl cover, one of the most widely produced of all time. During the Cultural Revolution, it became virtually mandatory to own and carry one.

In his foreword to *Mao's Little Red Book*, Lin Biao wrote of Mao, "A genius like him has been seen only once in several thousand years in China, and in several hundred years throughout the world."

Back then nearly all Chinese people—especially the young—took such claims as the absolute truth. The lyrics of a popular song in those years went like this:

Heaven is big, the Earth is vast,
But the kindness the Party shows us is bigger than both;

Mother loves me, Father loves me,
But Chairman Mao loves me even more.

Socialism is the greatest, and class love the most
profound;
Mao's ideas are a treasure;
We will fight anyone who stands against them.

Young students like me took to belting out this song over
and over, singing until our throats burned and our voices
grew hoarse. To us, Chairman Mao came first, with our
parents coming in a close—but definite—second.

My school, the Beijing Foreign Languages School,
enrolled many students from high-level government families.
My classmates were therefore better informed than most
people. Long before the Cultural Revolution officially
kicked off in August 1966, the classrooms and hallways
teemed with rumors that our Party was infested with
revisionists, that capitalism was trying to make a comeback,
and that someone was trying to seize power from our Great
Leader, Chairman Mao.

These rumors were a bolt out of the blue, leaving many
of us tearful, angry, and sleepless. Some of us even burst into
painful cries in each other's arms. Someone had dared to
defy Chairman Mao? It was indefensible.

The concept of class struggle figured heavily in our
studies. Mao once advised his niece, Mao Yuanxin: "Take
class struggle as a major in your studies. Unless you have
understood what class struggle means, you can't say you are
ready to graduate from college. Even if you have, I will
arrange a follow-up course for you." With this advice
designated as a "supreme instruction," class struggle was

inserted into every school curriculum and at every level of study.

Like my schoolmates, I kept class struggle in mind whenever I met other people. The rich were selfish and cruel; the poor, conversely, were supremely good. Class enemies, I thought, were lurking all around me. I had to be vigilant.

Once, a peasant woman came to speak to my class. Dressed in tattered clothes, she began to tell of the miseries she had suffered before the founding of New China. During a famine caused by crop failure, a landowner had refused to waive her family's rent on the land, and her family could do nothing but flee their home, begging their way into exile. They had nearly died.

This was clearly not the first time she had told this story, but the woman did a very nice job of it, punctuating her performance with genuine whimpers and cries.

As she spoke the room went totally quiet. Tears sprang from students' eyes, and some of the girls even broke into painful sobs.

All at once the teacher who'd organized the woman's visit stood up and pumped his right fist in the air. "Bear in mind the suffering we had in the old society," he shouted, "and the hatred we had against our class enemies! Down with the viciousness of the old society!"

At this everyone in the room—faculty and students alike—raised their fists and chorused the same exact words. And then came this fierce and familiar chant: "Long live the Great Leader!"

★★★

The theme of class struggle hovered over every schoolroom in the country. The blackboard in my classroom, and all the other classrooms at school, originally bore the slogan: "Study for the Sake of the Country." Nobody knew why this slogan was revised to read "Study for the Sake of Revolution," but no one questioned the change.

One day I walked into the classroom and noticed two new phrases written on the wall at the far end of the room: "Yes to the Proletariat" and "No to Capitalism." Our teacher explained the rules for a new class activity: "'Yes' means to publicize proletarian thought and 'No' means to eliminate capitalist ideologies." A rectangular section was marked with shiny red paper strips and cut evenly into two parts by a green strip in the middle. The left side was reserved for praise and the right side for criticism.

We students took to this new game at once. Although the "Yes" section had more notes, the "No" section was much more entertaining. A girl in a pair of nylon knee-socks was the first to appear in the "No" section, followed by another girl with a stylish hairstyle. Both girls were cited for their "bourgeois inclinations."

But the most innocent victim was the classmate sitting next to me. The boy absolutely adored stewed pork with dry-salted potherb mustard. Because no such dish was ever served in the school canteen, his mother wrapped up some pork in an empty medicine box for him to enjoy at school. Ours was a boarding school—we were released home only on weekends—so he had to parse out his treat carefully, picking out just a little for each meal. For reasons I never quite understood, he and his favorite dish found their way into the "No" column, joining others charged with harboring bourgeois inclinations. No one was permitted to challenge, much less resist, such designations. One day in my political education class, the lecturer told us how capitalists exploited factory workers in the old society. When he finished, one student stood up to ask a question.

"My mother works at a watch factory," he said, "and each worker produces many watches a month but is paid very little. Is this also exploitation?"

"No," the teacher replied. "A capitalist owned the factory in the old society, and so the money all went into his pocket. Factories are now government-owned and the money they make goes to the state—it's two totally different things."

The student wasn't satisfied. "Do you mean," he pursued, "that the government is exploiting workers nowadays?"

"The answer to that question is also no," the teacher replied patiently. "The money made as revenue is to be used for the country's construction and people's social benefits. Our system is 'from the people and for the people.'"

The next day, several new lines had appeared on the back wall, accusing that inquisitive student of "slandering socialism and defending capitalism." The teacher in charge of our class was very kind, for he removed these writings from the "No" section before any administrators or visiting government officials could see them.

∗∗∗

I had no idea about this at the time, but later I would come to understand that the pursuit of truth begins with doubt. The British philosopher Bertrand Russell writes in his *Sceptical Essays*: "According to primary school textbooks in Germany, Napoleon was frustrated by the sheer power of Germany; according to primary school textbooks in Britain, it was by the power of the United Kingdom. Both textbooks should be put side by side for primary school pupils to learn from." At the time, some people disagreed with Russell's suggestion. Students would be confused by the varying viewpoints, they argued. "It's when your pupils begin to doubt," Russell insisted, "that your instruction has been successful."

The education we received in those years left no room for us to question what we were learning. None. Your only option was to ingest what you were given and to believe everything you were told. Anything short of total credulity marked you as being against the revolutionary cause.

Education fashioned China's youth into die-hard revolutionaries, but when the Cultural Revolution finally ended, many of us discovered that all that coercion and complacency had left a very bitter taste in our mouths.

Yuanmingyuan Imperial Garden, the largest of its kind in the world, was twice attacked by foreign armies. The site was pillaged and set afire in 1860 with only a few buildings remaining. In 1901, these were destroyed by the Eight-Power Allied forces. A hundred years later, it became the birthplace of the country's first Red Guards.

A Red Guard armband. Most Red Guard wear armbands and yellow army uniforms.

FROM HISTORY'S RUINS

"LET'S GO TO THE SUMMER PALACE," MY SISTER SUGGESTED ONE
Sunday in May 1966.

We'd always been a close family and the move to Beijing
had strengthened our bond. During the week my older
brother Xu Yang and I were away at boarding school, but
on the weekends we all made a point of spending time
together.

As usual, when Father asked what we'd like to do on
Saturday, it was my little sister Si Yan who spoke up first,
this time suggesting a visit to the stately Summer Palace.

Xu Yang shot me a knowing look—or maybe it was a
look of sympathy. We'd already been to the Summer Palace
a few times, and he knew better than anybody that I would
rather stay home for a quiet weekend of reading. But we had
a family rule: Anything we did on weekends, we did
together. Except for him, that is. Since turning eighteen, Xu
Yang had at last gained permission from our father to do as
he pleased.

I sighed and sank deeper into my seat. My sister Si Yan was Father's favorite, which meant we usually did what she wanted on the weekend.

Not this time.

Father turned to me. "Do you really want to be a diplomat someday?" he asked me, his eyes steady on mine. His voice was low and serious.

I nodded.

"In that case," he continued, "you should see a place you've never been to before. Every diplomat should see it, even a diplomat-to-be."

I leaned forward in my chair, my interest instantly piqued. "Where's that?"

"The Yuanmingyuan Imperial Garden," he said. "The *Old* Summer Palace."

Father loved history, and I shared his enthusiasm. He'd told me many stories about the Old Imperial Palace—its once-majestic mansions and sumptuous gardens—and I'd wanted to see it ever since.

I was thrilled, but when I looked over at my sister I saw that her mouth had curled into a frown.

"Trust me," I told her, "Yuanmingyuan used to be the most beautiful garden in the world."

Her mind must have fastened onto the "most beautiful garden in the world" part while skipping past the "used to be" that preceded it. She blinked her eyes in agreement and smiled.

The Old Summer Palace it would be.

✮✮✮

Like the Phantom Islands of old science-fiction novels, the Red Guards seemed to come out of nowhere, only to disappear suddenly and without a trace. Whenever they are mentioned today, the first things that come to mind are their formidable powers of destruction and their determination to crush anything in their path. Just days after they were established, they astounded the world. Time, however, changes everything. Eventually the Red Guards proved just as short-lived as a meteor streaking across the night sky, lasting only a couple of years during the lone decade of the Cultural Revolution. Today, they've faded into a blurred impression of frenzied mobs, painted green faces, and ferocious fangs.

For me, however, the Red Guards would prove a force as strong as fate, and although I didn't know it for a time, I was present at the very site of their birth in May 1966.

We set out for the Old Summer Palace early in the morning, my mother, father, sister, and I. Neither the new Summer Palace nor the old one was far from our apartment. All we needed to do was take a short bus ride on Route Thirty-Two, and then a short walk to the left or right from the Peking University bus station to Yuanmingyuan.

The magic of Beijing was still new to me in those days. Once we boarded the bus, I pressed my forehead against the glass window and peered out onto the city. The vast length and breadth of Eternal Peace Boulevard, which ran east to west through the city; the clamor and chaos of the alleyways and the stately gardens and parks; the endless song of the cicadas, the dust that flew in from the western deserts, and the sharp fragrance of the pines—Beijing thrilled and fascinated me.

My mother had plans of her own that day. While Si Yan, Father, and I toured the grounds of the Old Summer Palace, she would drop in on a friend at Tsinghua University and collect a book of piano scores. This was how we gained access to Tsinghua Middle School, which was a boarding school like my own.

That day the campus was much quieter than usual. Even on Sundays, students could be seen here and there, milling about the grounds and playing basketball. Not today. The quiet was only on the surface; beneath it lay a devastating gunpowder barrel just waiting for the strike of a match. That strike was at the ready, for at that moment a number of students were gathering secretly at the Old Summer Palace of Yuanmingyuan, ready to set it ablaze.

There are different stories told about that day. Luo Xiaohai, one of those involved, asserted that it "happened during the afternoon of May 29, when the representatives of different sides from different classes of the school arrived for a meeting at Yuanmingyuan, at which the name 'Red Guards' was officially established."

But the account left by Bu Dahua, who would soon emerge as one of the principal Red Guards, suggests a less tidy sequence of events: "The organization of the Red Guards was not officially announced as being established on that day. The only thing that was agreed upon was that 'unified action' be undertaken from that day on." Wang Ming, similarly closely involved, recalled, "It was a meeting of people with identical views, a meeting that was not exclusive at all." Another attendee, Song Bailin, later marked the occasion in his diary: "Some of us went for a meeting at Yuanmingyuan. We founded the Red Guards and made a plan for counterattacks."

According to Yan Yangsheng: "The May 29 meeting was held to coordinate people with different views. During another meeting held the next day, the name 'Red Guards' was established for any action we took part in, and we started putting up big-character posters from that day on."

Representatives from the different groups all agreed, however, that the May 29 meeting constituted the first time they'd all come together, and that it took place two days *before* the publication of the infamous *People's Daily* story praising Nie Yuanzi's "big-character poster." This "before" would always mean a lot to the Red Guards. Nie Yuanzi's poster offered a searing indictment of the status quo, but the Red Guards considered themselves the Cultural Revolution's advance guard.

There are also different versions of how the name "Red Guards" came to be. By one account, on the evening of May 29, a group of students—Bu Dahua, Wang Ming, Luo Xiaohai and Zhang Xiaobing among them—met in the ruins of the Yuanmingyuan Imperial Garden by climbing over a wall from their school. They were absolutely determined to create a revolutionary organization of their own. As their model they took the Young Guards from the Soviet Union's patriotic war against the Nazis. These students were already on the school's blacklist and had also been identified as troublemakers by the local police. They'd therefore have to proceed in strictest secrecy.

When the discussion reached the question of just how to sign the big-character posters they were about to compose, one of them put forth an ingenious idea: They'd call themselves the Red Guards. The term had first appeared during the October Revolution of 1917, when armed workers successfully seized power from the czar. Lenin spoke highly of the original Red Guards, describing them as "a revolutionary fortress."

And that's what they would be: China's own revolutionary fortress. "*Red* means revolutionary," said the student at the ruins of Yuanmingyuan, "and we are Red Guards and soldiers. Our mission is to protect the Party Central Committee and Chairman Mao." Everyone was happy with this name, so they raised their right arms in a very solemn manner to read a vow specially written for the occasion: "We are the guards of the red authorities. The Party Central Committee and Chairman Mao are behind us. Our mission is to liberate mankind and Mao Thought is our final instruction. We are willing to fight to the death for the Party Central Committee and our Great Leader Chairman Mao."

This version of the story, however, would be contradicted by the famous writer Zhang Chengzhi. According to Zhang, he had used the name much earlier than May 29, 1966. He had signed his "small-character posters" at primary school with the words "Red Guard," illustrating them with a soldier on horseback. He always penciled the image in red.

In the end, these details weren't nearly as important as the place the group chose for their secret meeting that night: the ruins of the Old Summer Palace. In this, the emergence of the Red Guards was related, albeit distantly, to the activities of the United States.

Tsinghua Middle School, which was affiliated with the prestigious Tsinghua University, stood right on the ruins of the Yuanmingyuan Imperial Garden—once the largest (at nearly 1,000 acres) and most beautiful of its kind in the world. It had taken roughly 150 years to complete this "garden of all gardens." Its destruction came first at the hands of the Anglo-French Allied forces in 1860. After looting one-and-a-half million priceless treasures, they set the whole garden on fire. Then, in 1900, the eight-nation-strong Allied Forces descended on China, ravaging the garden a second time. The United States was one of those eight, and this time the Old Summer Palace was laid completely to waste.

But the connection between the Red Guards and the United States went further than that. Tsinghua University, previously known as the Tsinghua School, was founded and built by the U.S. government with the "boxer indemnities" paid by the Chinese government. The founders of the Red Guards organization had been students at the middle school affiliated with Tsinghua University. Today, Tsinghua is one of the two most revered institutes of higher education in China—but whenever the Chinese people take a closer look at the history of Tsinghua, they react with a mix of gratitude and resentment.

The ruins of Yuanmingyuan still come to mind whenever I think of the Red Guards. The Guards themselves would destroy a great number of cultural and historical sites throughout the country in the ensuing years, but it was here, at this site symbolizing a vanquished and bitter past, that they chose to begin their ruinous campaign.

Standing shoulder to shoulder with my father, gazing at the ruins of the Old Summer Palace, what I saw was a scene of complete desolation. Slabs of the original palace buildings had long since collapsed and now lay scattered in the grass. The land had been reclaimed for farming, but on that day the soil looked coarse and barren. The area surrounding the two middle schools on the property, Tsinghua and Beijing 101, was a wasteland, empty but for a few desolate cottages and huts.

Later I would understand that by taking me to the Old Summer Palace, Father wanted me to see both what our country had lost and what more we could still lose—what we were, in fact, already losing by forgetting the past. In those moments, however, I only felt sadness and confusion. As we picked our way through the ruins, we passed a number of students. I didn't pay them much notice, but they were there, striding past us in pairs and in groups, gathering in the woods—the country's very first Red Guards.

"What Are You Up To During the Cultural Revolution?" The infamous, first "big-character poster" of the Cultural Revolution, written by Nie Yuanzi and others.

Rebels putting up big-character posters.

REVOLUTIONARY INK

Nobody who lived through the Cultural Revolution would ever forget them: big-character posters. They covered anything and everything in those days. More than any other symbol, these posters embodied the strangeness and cruelty of the era's politics. For many years, a big-character poster could end a career, if not a life.

The term "big-character poster" generally refers to the revolutionary slogans that were inscribed onto huge sheets of paper and posted in public places during the revolution. In some respects, big-character posters constituted the first real opportunity for free expression within the country's legal systems. They were considered "the best route to a people's democracy" and "a very effective weapon of a new generation."

These posters could spring up anywhere, in any color and in any size. Even the form of expression was entirely up to the writer's whim: the text might be a short passage from a book, an essay, a slogan, a poem, or even a cartoon. But while the format varied widely, the content always aimed to do one thing: to shock.

No one was spared; anyone's dignity and privacy could be violated. Taking a person's remarks out of context, grossly exaggerating their actions—even slander or libel didn't raise eyebrows so long as the writer claimed "a revolutionary stance" or "a revolutionary purpose." The only risk, should you have engaged in this practice, was that someone would retaliate by writing a poster to take you down, too.

Back then, you saw an ocean of big-character posters wherever you went, both in the city and the countryside. The school I attended was no exception. They could be seen all over campus, inside classrooms and restrooms and in every hallway. When there wasn't a square inch of empty space left anywhere, new posters were simply papered over the old ones.

Paper was in short supply during those years—the paper-making industry had been pushed to overload—which made the ubiquity of the posters even more astonishing. Due to the insufficient supply of materials, even toilet paper was hard to find in some places. A relative of mine told me how, when he once got the news that a small shop outside a paper-making mill had just received some toilet paper in stock, he rushed there early in the morning to stand for several hours in a long queue before obtaining five rolls. He then danced his way home with those fine trophies.

And yet, despite the scarcity of paper, the posters cropped up in every corner of the country: government departments, businesses, factories, even threshing grounds in the countryside. From beginning to end, the big-character phenomena lasted twenty-odd years. In that time they'd cause untold tragedies.

✷✷✷

The first big-character poster to gain a national audience—and the one that stoked the first fires of revolution—materialized at Peking University. Written by seven university lecturers—Nie Yuanzi being one of them—it appeared on May 25, 1966, on the eastern wall of the big cafeteria on the university campus. The initial motive was to launch a complaint against the university administration, yet this pair of butterfly wings started a huge political storm that nobody could stop.

Two months after the poster's appearance, during a meeting of the Central Committee of the Communist Party of China (CCP), Mao said, "I didn't expect the huge impact this poster would have after being broadcast on the radio." He spoke highly of it, describing it as "the first Marxist big-character poster across the country."

The two most important mouthpieces of the Communist Party, the *People's Daily* and *Red Flag,* confirmed the big-character poster's importance. "Like a match," they asserted, "[the poster] lit the raging flames of the proletarian Cultural Revolution, a mass movement against a handful of leading capitalist road-takers inside the Party."

I saw that infamous poster three days after it was first put up.

I'd planned to trade some books with Liu Li, a classmate whose father was a faculty member at Peking University. Liu Li and his family lived on campus, and that day was the first time I ever set foot on the university grounds. Although cycling was allowed, I wanted to show my respect to this venerable place of higher learning, so instead of riding my bike I hopped off and walked alongside it.

To me, these were the most sacred of grounds. Founded in 1898 under the name of the Imperial University of Peking, this was the first national institute of higher learning in China, signifying the advent of higher education in the modern sense. With its many illustrious alumni—Mao himself had once worked there as a librarian—Peking University was in every sense at the center of China's cultural and ideological development. The path I was taking, I thought to myself as I walked my bike that day, must have been trod by many great people. My feet might have fallen in Mao's very own footsteps—who knew?

After exchanging books, Liu Li saw me out to the door. We were still chatting when suddenly we heard loud shouts coming from outside.

"It's happening again!" Liu Li said, pulling at my bike to stop me from leaving. "Why don't we go and take a look?"

Not yet fourteen, I couldn't resist the prospect of witnessing some excitement. I parked my bike, and together Liu Li and I made our way toward the center of campus.

From a distance I saw a huge crowd gathering. Several hundred people had come together, most of them young students, but also some adults who were obviously faculty members. In groups of three or four, they were discussing—

no, heatedly debating—something of great importance.

As Liu Li and I got closer, I saw that a group of men had surrounded a woman and were taunting her. She shot back a bitter answer, though I couldn't make out exact words.

How could a group of men be bullying a woman? And at such a venerated place of higher learning?

He must have noticed my confusion because Liu Li said, "That's Nie Yuanzi, a very ambitious woman, according to my father. She's the one who wrote that big-character poster criticizing the university administration. She even went so far as to name names!"

That was the first time I saw the notorious Nie Yuanzi. She was an ordinary-looking woman in her forties, with short hair and glasses. Within just a couple of days she'd become notorious throughout the country, a university leader, and, before long, one of the five major leaders of the Red Guards. Of course I couldn't know that yet, but as I took in the scene that day, I admired her courage and composure as she confronted such a large group of angry men who shot furious questions at her.

People continued to argue hotly, each side supremely confident that it had the truth on their side. Some of the things they said, about "the working team" or "Lu Ping" (whom I later found out was the university president), baffled me. I had no clue what was going on.

Eventually I grew bored, so I turned away, meaning to leave.

It was at that moment that Liu Li made a surprising remark: "My father says this woman will soon be finished."

That stopped me cold. Now I *had* to read that big-character poster of hers.

The poster had been tacked to the outside wall of the school's main cafeteria. By the time we got there, a big crowd had gathered before it. I managed to squeeze through to the very front.

I'd thought it would be just one sheet of paper, but I was wrong. It was comprised of seven white sheets, aligned in two rolls, four on top and three at the bottom. On either side the poster was flanked with slogans configured to look like protective Red Guards. One side read, "Long live the great proletarian Cultural Revolution." The other read, "Long live Chairman Mao's revolutionary line." Many big-character posters had been put up around it in rebuttal, vying for people's attention.

The poster had appeared three days before, Liu told me. During the afternoon of the first day, he said, more than a thousand big-character posters had appeared in retaliation. To many people, Nie Yuanzi had gotten everything backwards. She was seeking to counteract the Party and the revolution. She deserved to be punished, they said.

Liu Li explained that the title took aim at the Beijing municipal government official in charge of university affairs; the second name belonged to the secretary of the university's Party Committee and the university president; and the third referred to the secretary's assistant.

The poster began in a very harsh tone: "When the nation is engaged actively in the Cultural Revolution; when the nation has an unbounded love of Chairman Mao and equally unbounded hatred against the sinister coun-terrevolutionary and anti-socialist capitalist roaders inside the Party; when the nation is starting an all-round attack against the enemy and doing everything it can to protect the Party Central Committee and Chairman Mao; our Peking University is as dead as a doornail, taking no action at all. The requests to join the struggle from teachers and students alike are ignored. Why? Something suspicious is going on here."

After a long list of "facts" to support its argument, and an equally long list of rebukes, came this: "Why did you 'guide' people not to hold revolutionary meetings, not to write big-character posters, and with rules made in haste to suppress people in any revolutionary actions? Why are you against the revolution of the masses?"

I squinted to make out the rest of what was written on the poster. "We are firmly opposed to your practices," the poster continued. "What kind of posts are you holding, and for whom are you acting? What kind of people are you? What are you up to? Your evil-doing is as bright as the daylight; nothing can stop history in its progress—it's daydreaming, the actions of a fool!"

Nie Yuanzi's big-character poster closed with a call to action: "It's time for all revolutionary intellectuals to rise up and fight; let's hold high the great banner of Mao's thoughts and be united; let's rally around the Party Central Committee and Chairman Mao. We must break the control of revisionism, frustrate their schemes and wipe off all kinds of monsters and devils in a thorough, firm and absolute manner. Down with anti-revolutionaries; down with revisionists of the Khrushchev kind. We will push socialist revolution to the end." Three shrill slogans appeared at the very end: "Protect the Party Central Committee!"; "Protect

Mao's Thought!"; and "Protect the Proletarian Dictatorship!" I saw that seven people, all from the philosophy department faculty, had signed their names. Nie Yuanzi's was the first signature.

I was quite distraught on my way home from Peking University that day. What Nie Yuanzi had written sounded quite reasonable to me, but so did the claims of her detractors. The education I had received over the previous years had come in just one voice and followed one path of reasoning, but on that day, I encountered something quite different and new—two groups of people standing in opposition to each other. Both claimed to be revolutionary, but their arguments were completely different. I had no way at all to tell which side was right.

I wasn't the only one thrown into confusion.

Nie Yuanzi's poster had the top level of the CCP quite nervous. They immediately initiated a series of actions to offset its impact. Liu Shaoqi, the state president and Vice Chairman of the CCP Central Committee, heard about the poster the day it appeared. That night, he called a meeting with Zhou Enlai, the Premier of the State Council, and the leader of the CCP Central Committee's head group for the Cultural Revolution. They discussed what should be done to prevent the situation from escalating if students took to the streets. They decided that Li Xuefeng, assisted by the Minister of Higher Education and the leader of the State Council's Foreign Affairs Office, should go to Peking University and get the situation there under control.

Li Xuefeng had just been appointed the secretary of the CCP Beijing Committee. Entrusted with this mission at such a difficult moment, he rushed to the university that same night. The loudspeakers on campus woke everyone up with a very brief notice: the university's Party Committee members must appear immediately in the auditorium. There, Li Xuefeng reiterated the rules of the Party and the State: differentiation had to be made between people inside and outside the Party; no Party members should create any big-character posters, and instead students should try their best to stop other people from doing so. Later a number of rooms on campus were vacated to store big-character posters. These rooms were to be watched closely by special personnel.

As a longtime Communist Party member, Nie Yuanzi was seriously reprimanded at the meeting. On the following day, a vice president of the university was sent to speak with her, asking her to re-examine her behavior and to remove her poster. Nie Yuanzi refused.

She'd soon gain a powerful ally. Five days later, Mao read the report about Nie Yuanzi's poster. At this point he had withdrawn to the "second line," leaving "first-line matters" to Liu Shaoqi, his assistant and successor. But Mao was seriously disappointed with Liu's ideas on governance. One of his purposes for initiating the Cultural Revolution was to keep China from undergoing "peaceful evolution from socialism back to capitalism." Much to his dismay, he found few supporters inside the Party, and his Cultural Revolution seemed to have stalled. Under pressure, he had searched high and low for a way to engage the masses from the bottom up. His wife, Madame Mao, would eventually announce Mao's strategy from Tiananmen Tower during the second year of the Cultural Revolution: "Chairman Mao thought about this for a long time until he found this way, the Cultural Revolution, to mobilize the masses and to overthrow the capitalist roaders inside the Party."

Nie Yuanzi's poster presented Mao with an opportunity. He was in Hangzhou when he first saw this big-character poster. He made what would be a brilliant move: he wrote to Kang Sheng and Chen Boda, two leaders of the Cultural Revolution's head group, and announced, "We must broadcast this poster from Xinhua News Agency and publish it in all newspapers across the country. The counterrevolutionary fortress of Peking University is collapsing."

He wouldn't suffer a minute's delay, so he telephoned Kang Sheng, instructing him to broadcast the poster's text that very evening.

China National Radio did as Mao commanded.

I woke with a start the next morning.

Voices boomed from the loudspeakers across the street from our apartment building. Few people had access to a radio, much less a television, and the few televisions in Beijing, Shanghai, and Guangzhou carried just a few official programs. If the Party or government wanted to communicate with people, radio stations and loudspeakers were the fastest and most powerful method. The loudspeaker at the university across the street often sprang to life in the middle of the night, jolting everyone from sleep. What would be called extreme noise pollution today was a normal part of life back in those years. Without loudspeakers or access to a radio, you simply had no idea what was going on.

I sat up and listened more carefully. After a while I figured out that the broadcast was an article from the *People's Daily*. It praised the big-character poster displayed at Peking University and called for more revolutionary actions.

I slipped out of bed and hurried into the front room. Father was about to leave for work, but he now returned and sat back down at the kitchen table. He asked my mother to brew him a cup of his favorite black tea. He sat motionless, listening intently to the blaring loudspeakers.

I was thrilled. I'd just seen this poster a couple of days before at Peking University and now I was listening to it on the radio. I felt like I was part of a momentous event.

Those were still happy and carefree days for me. An organization of the Red Guards had been set up in the middle school affiliated with Peking University, and other middle schools in the area, including mine, soon did the same. My classmates followed all the latest political happenings. Nobody had the patience to sit still in a classroom, listening to lectures, and doing lessons—I certainly didn't.

Then, all at once, classes were suspended. The administration seemed unable to do anything about it. Left to our own devices, my classmates and I were all hoping something exciting would soon happen and that we could be a part of it.

Now it seemed that something was happening—something really big.

I didn't want to miss out on this latest development. When the loudspeaker finally quieted, I sprang to my feet and made for the door.

But before I could leave, Father called out, "Go and see if today's *People's Daily* has arrived yet!"

My father was very strict with us at home. Everything he said was an instruction. I had no choice but to run down the stairs and wait for the postman to deliver the newspaper.

A short time later, when Father had finished reading the paper, I glanced at the front page. The article I'd just heard on the broadcast appeared on the front page, along with a strange headline running above the text: "Sweep Away All Monsters and Demons." I'd encountered this ominous phrase before in *Strange Tales from a Chinese Studio*, a novel by Pu Songling, one of China's classic writers. All the tales in that book were about supernatural spirits, and I couldn't understand why they'd come up in a newspaper article.

"Why are they referring to monsters and devils here?" I asked Father.

He didn't answer.

"Who are they talking about?" I asked.

He still didn't answer, leaving me even more bewildered. Although he could be harsh with us, Father always had the patience to answer any question we posed. But on that day, he seemed quite different from his usual self.

He must have something on his mind, I told myself, something very unpleasant.

I didn't ask Father any more questions that morning. Instead, I dug for answers in my own mind.

I was very thirsty for knowledge in those days. Like a dried-up sponge, I absorbed anything and everything. Seeing the look on my father's face, I felt the same worry I'd experienced after reading the poster at Peking University. I had to find out more about what was going on in the country.

That day I started collecting newspaper clippings. The copy of the *People's Daily* with "Sweep Away All Monsters and Demons" became the first in my collection.

Nie Yuanzi's big-character poster was like a stone thrown into a quiet pond. No, it was much more than that. Together with the radio broadcast, the two events were like two nuclear explosions, sending shock waves across the country.

The foreboding tone of the *People's Daily* article, which described the situation as "very grave," caught the rest of the Party leaders by surprise. In an article titled "Cheers to the First Big-Character Poster at Peking University," the university was denounced as counterrevolutionary. An anti-socialist fortress.

There was more: the Communist Party of China, it claimed, had split into two parties—a true Communist Party and a false one. The ideas expressed in the article were razor-sharp: "Whatever kind of party or organization you are talking about, we cannot help but reach this conclusion— your party is not the genuine CCP...It is false and revisionist and your organization is actually an anti-Party clique."

The warning was clear: When you see something wrong

in the Party, do not hesitate to rise up and revolt.

All the top leaders of the CCP understood the significance of Mao's approval of Nie Yuanzi's poster: it was a call to revolution. What they didn't understand was *why* Mao approved it. Chen Yi, a member of the CCP Political Bureau and vice premier, asked Zhou Enlai, "Why didn't we receive any notice about an important matter like this?" He didn't know either, replied Zhou Enlai, claiming he was informed only minutes before the broadcast. Liu Shaoqi and Deng Xiaoping also claimed to have been caught off guard.

The reaction from Peking University was by far the strongest. In the early evening of June 1, all the loudspeakers on campus barked an urgent notice: Everyone, student and faculty alike, must listen to the very important news that was about to be broadcast on China National Radio. The "news" was People Daily's endorsement of Nie Yuanzi's big-character poster. Radically different responses streaked through campus—some people were wild with excitement, while others were deeply concerned. Nie Yuanzi and the other big-poster signatories had faced a tumultuous few days; now they were overjoyed. Her opponents, meanwhile, were totally furious. At that point, nobody knew that the article had Mao's approval. Before the broadcast came to an end, the campus exploded with angry shouting. "Refuse the arrogance of both the radio station and *People's Daily!*" Dozens of new big-character posters appeared overnight, covering the old ones with fresh rage.

★★★

In the end, Mao's bold move served his purposes well.

In the weeks following the *People's Daily* broadcast, people flooded into Peking University day and night for a chance to see the poster first-hand. According to university reports, for a period of time the campus averaged more than 100,000 visitors a day.

More universities followed Peking University's example, dragging their own presidents and deans down, who now faced public humiliation. Party organizations at all levels stopped functioning and the situation spun out of control. This was precisely what Mao expected. His strategy was to achieve "great order from great disorder under the heavens" and the big-poster maelstrom brought about exactly the kind of great disorder he had planned.

Buildings in the classical Chinese style at Peking University.

THE SPECTACLE

THE VICTIMS WERE ON THEIR KNEES WITH THEIR ARMS TWISTED behind their backs. Tall paper hats had been set on their heads and cardboard signs hung from their necks. Black characters streaked across the signs, the letters highlighted with red ink for emphasis. I stepped closer to make out the words, but it was no use. I was pinned back by the crowd and I couldn't get closer to the stand. All at once the loudspeakers boomed to life, and with that the students encircled the platform, their faces transfigured by hate.

Violence now sparked from campus to campus. Peking University proved a forerunner in many respects. As the huge and almost uncontrollable political energy inspired by the big-character posters grew, revolutionary fervor spread through the whole university campus. Students began to torture their instructors, which only spurred more violence at other campuses across the country. The first such case occurred on June 18. Unfortunately, I would be a part of it.

My brother and I each had a small bookcase at home, and over the years some world-famous classic novels had mysteriously migrated from my father's shelves to ours. After trading books with my classmate Liu Li that first time, he discovered my treasure trove. Soon afterward, he paid me a visit.

"A lot is going on at Peking University," he told me excitedly when we got to my room. Just yesterday, he continued, students from the department of physics had secretly held their dean and his assistants up for public humiliation. They'd been paraded through the streets with tall paper hats on their heads.

Liu Li used the words "monsters" and "devils" to refer to the victims. I felt a mix of fascination and horror. "What about tomorrow?" I asked. "Do you think anything like that will happen again tomorrow?"

"I'm not sure," Liu Li said, "but on my way here I did see some people putting up a 'devil stand' in front of a school building."

I felt my eyes widen with interest. It was settled—I made up my mind there and then. I would go see these evildoers in the flesh.

There was only one problem, and it was a big one: Father. Ever since my first visit to Peking University, I was desperate to return to the campus, but my father forbade it.

"It's chaos over there," he said. "It's simply not safe for you to go."

I had one choice: I'd have to make up an excuse. The lie I finally told my father was the most impossible one for him to refuse. "The working team at my school told us to go to Peking University," I said. "They want us discuss what we see there after we return."

Father opened, then closed his mouth. My lie had worked. He had no choice but to let me go. I felt a pang of guilt, but for the moment I pushed it away.

✮✮✮

On June 18, 1966, I stepped onto the campus of Peking University for the second time and saw something I didn't expect and would never forget.

It was a very pleasant day, sunny and warm. I hitched a ride to campus on the back of my friend Chen Lu's bicycle. Fewer people were around this time. From their peculiar clothes, I guessed some of them had come to Beijing from other parts of the country, most likely to see Nie Yuanzi's now-notorious big-character poster.

The campus was enormous, but because I'd been there once before I could find my way around fairly easily. It was Chen Lu's first time on the campus, however, so I led the way, walking slightly ahead.

Weiming Lake was the very picture of beauty and tranquility that day: rippling water, willow branches dancing in the breeze, and a gentle green slope rising in the distance.

After a time I threw a look over my shoulder to make sure

Chen Lu was behind me. I saw that his mouth was hanging open in awe.

"Amazing, isn't it?" I asked.

"Amazing!" he answered, his eyes still on the lake.

I dreamed of attending Peking University one day and had researched its history thoroughly. I'd been surprised to learn that this quintessentially Chinese-style campus had actually been designed by an American architect. The reason for this was simple: the Christian missionaries and organizations who came to China wanted to build a university, and to reduce any opposition to their plans they compromised by adopting Chinese architectural features in their designs for the campus.

Set amid luxuriant trees, the buildings were richly ornamented, with carved beams and painted rafters. The American architect Henry Murphy had deftly integrated classical Chinese elements throughout the university. The buildings seemed both stately and full of life.

Chen Lu and I were busy admiring the campus when we came upon something wholly unexpected. Loud voices boomed from the loudspeakers, and we hurried toward them to make out what was being said. As we approached the loudspeakers, we came upon a pair of six- or seven-story dorm-like buildings. These buildings encircled a horseshoe-shaped stretch of open space, which was now filled with people. They faced a wooden stage that had been erected there.

My heart hammered against my chest. More people were headed toward the stage, I realized, and in each crowd were some wearing tall paper hats. Their arms were twisted behind their backs and they struggled to keep up.

"They're professors," I heard some people around me saying.

I couldn't believe my ears or my eyes. These professors were the "monsters" and "devils" who people had been talking about? It didn't make any sense.

I squeezed into the crowd and managed to get to the front. I was very close to the stage now and had a clear view of the proceedings. Several people had been forced to their knees. Their arms were still twisted in the students' grasps and their heads pressed almost to the ground while their buttocks were pushed up in the air. Later I would learn that this humiliating position spread to other schools and took on the name "jet-propelled style."

Posters hung from the victims' necks. Their names were spelled out and boldly crossed out in red ink. They were all motionless as their "crimes" were announced by young students. One girl was holding a female teacher by the hair. It must have been very painful, but the teacher dared not move. I could see her eyes filling with tears.

I became afraid then. I didn't believe in witchcraft or spells, in devils or demons. But I did believe in evil deeds— and in madness. As the students descended on their victims, my impulse was to run away as quickly and silently as I could.

Years later, I read an article about what happened on that day. Ma Shengxiang, then a student in the history department, painted this gruesome picture of the day's events:

A stand, big enough to hold dozens of people, had been constructed outside Building 38 at the corner outside its eastern exit. . .Each [target] had a tall paper hat on their head, and because there weren't enough for everyone, baskets full of used toilet paper were brought from nearby public restrooms. Some baskets were made with iron wire, which cut their flesh when pressed down on their heads. Blood could be seen on their faces. Some had black ink painted on their faces—what a miserable sight. When [a person's] turn came to be criticized, they were forced to their knees, head pushed low—and if anyone resisted, the students would begin to beat them until he or she gave up any resistance. On the cardboard notices hanging on their chests were written the lines 'revisionist seedling,' 'go-getter for the revisionist line in education,' 'reactionary gangster,' or 'royalist.' That meeting lasted for several hours, until someone from the working team came to stop it.

That day, dozens of victims were dragged about, insulted, and beaten. At one point, a large crowd gathered in the courtyard of the Chinese Language Department, shouting, "Give us Cheng Xiance!" This professor had already made a hasty escape, ducking into a ladies room. A kind-hearted woman inside the bathroom quickly hid the professor in her stall. The students found him anyway—and tortured him afterwards.

Well-known professors in the Chinese Language Department such as Wang Li, Wu Zuxiang, and Wang Yao were beaten with fists and sticks. A simple flash of a belt from one student pinned old professor Wang Yao on the ground. A basket of stinking toilet paper was brought out for Xiang Jingjie, the department's associate dean, before bottles of ink were splashed on his body. That night, his wife would apply layer after layer of medical salve to his bruised and bleeding back. Someone threw a rope around the neck of Hu Shouwen, a lecturer in the biological sciences department, and yanked it until he almost choked to death.

According to reports released almost a year later, fifty-six people were "struggled against" on that day in June 1966. Thirty-two of them were labeled "reactionary gang members," two as "reactionary students," and fourteen as "reactionaries of other kinds." Even at that time, eight of the targets were acknowledged as having been "wronged." Of the fifty-six, forty were from the school establishment or Party committees on different levels. Of the university's eighteen departments, instructors from sixteen were physically attacked. Only the departments of physics and geophysics suffered no victims. Oddly, the university president, Lu Ping, was spared. He'd already been dragged to meetings every day to be criticized and humiliated. By June 18, the self-styled revolutionaries had long since lost interest in him and had moved on to other targets.

Back at home, I went straight to bed. I hadn't had anything to eat or drink all day, but I couldn't face my family at the dinner table.

"Are you ill?" Mother asked, slipping into my room and

placing her palm on my forehead. Her voice was gentle and her brows furrowed with concern.

"No," I said. Part of me longed for her comfort, but for reasons I couldn't explain I wanted to be left alone. "I'm just tired," I said, pushing her hand away. "That's all it is." This much was true. I was exhausted—not physically, but mentally.

If you douse your body repeatedly with water, alternating between hot and cold water again and again, something eventually goes wrong within you. That was just how I felt that night. Over the previous five thousand years, Chinese people had valued education and educators above nearly all else. My mother had been a music teacher, and my father held undergraduate and graduate degrees. All my life I'd been taught to respect knowledge and those who disseminated it, and now that my belief had been shattered, my body registered the shock.

This isn't a dream, I told myself. *This is reality.* Somehow I had to face the events of the day squarely and make sense of what was happening around me.

"Class struggle," Mao once remarked, "should be remembered and talked about every day." I told myself that what I'd seen that day was just part of a larger, and essential, class struggle. *The monsters and devils were dragged onto the stand*, I thought. *They were wrongdoers who'd been hiding in our country's dark corners. Now that they'd shown their true form, they had to be routed out.* Students at Peking University were a select and talented group; surely they were more knowledgeable about this world than I was. Their actions must have been justified; their reasoning, I told myself, was simply beyond my feeble understanding.

A CAMPUS ABLAZE

ONE DAY, ON A PLEASANT LATE AFTERNOON, I WAS SITTING
outside near the basketball court reading *The Hunchback
of Notre Dame.* I'd reached the part where a group of
townspeople march the hunchback Quasimodo in the town
square and tie him to a post under the scorching sun. The
townspeople hurl all sorts of trash and insults at him.
Suddenly a beautiful, kind-hearted gypsy girl approaches
with water to quench his thirst.

"What's that book you're reading?" came a cold voice
behind me.

I'd been thoroughly engrossed in the story—just then I
was reading the passage describing Quasimodo's tears
of gratitude—but the voice from behind jolted me back
to reality.

I whipped around and saw that one of my teachers was
peering down at me. My face flushed. Before this, I'd been
reading a love scene between the heroine Esmeralda and

Phoebus de Chateaupers, the handsome captain of the king's archers. How long had the teacher been standing there? Had he been watching me as I read that part too?

"And how do you like the story?" the teacher asked after I told him the title of the book. Then he casually asked me about my family background. This teacher's one of the kind ones here, I thought to myself. There was nothing to worry about—I could speak freely with him. When he asked about my family, I told him about my parents, telling him about Father's work at the *Beijing Review* and even mentioning my mother's landlord family background.

"Someone in our class enjoys reading foreign novels more than revolutionary books," the teacher announced to the class the next day.

I hadn't given the exchange a second thought, but now my face reddened with shame. Though my name wasn't mentioned, it was obvious to everyone who the teacher was referring to.

"If this preference continues," he went on, his tone pointed and harsh, "such a student will unwittingly fall victim to capitalism, feudalism, and revisionism." At the end of this speech he cast a meaningful glance in my direction.

I felt like a mountain was about to fall on top of me. My classmates turned their eyes to me, knowing full well my love of reading. I felt too ashamed to show my face to them now. Worst of all was that I believed the teacher was right and I was wrong. He had cut straight to the point, I told myself. My vigilance on behalf of class struggle had faltered. How stupid I was, I chided myself.

From that point on, every time my eyes fell to my little

bookshelf at home, I felt the urge to throw away all the books there. But I was unable to do it. All I did was to keep reminding myself: "You can't read those anymore! Be strong, with a revolutionary will of steel!"

★★★

Tsinghua Middle School had turned into a barrel of explosives. The detonator came in the form of a big-character poster signed by the Red Guards.

Days before, Nie Yuanzi's famous big-character poster had appeared at Peking University. Similar acts were now widely encouraged. The students of Tsinghua Middle School composed a big-character poster entitled "Fight to Death for the Proletarian Dictatorship and Mao Thought" and mounted it inside the large classroom on the fifth floor. Every word was like a bullet shot at the school administration.

"Capitalist masters," the students wrote, "since you have provoked us, we are here to pick up the fight. We won't stop fighting until we have completely uprooted your black banners, destroyed your gangs, smashed your posts, and closed your black markets!"

After the glaring "Red Guards" at the bottom were the signatures of Bu Dahua, Wang Ming, and Luo Xiaohai, founders of the Red Guards movement. A space was left conspicuously blank beneath their signatures; this is where supporters were to add their names. The charisma of this poster was clearly just too much to resist—on that day alone, more than a hundred names were added to the poster.

In this way, the Red Guards spread into the nation's schools. Similar organizations under other names appeared overnight, but history had its own plans. Like a highly imaginative playwright, it pushed the plot toward unexpected turns.

The big-character poster written by Tsinghua Middle School students was taken very seriously by the municipal education department, which considered these students to be troublemakers. Their actions would never be tolerated. A blistering report on these students was issued and circulated throughout educational circles. This report turned out to be a catalyst—while the administrators meant it as a weapon to suppress opposing ideas from the student body, the effect was simply that more and more people came to know about the Red Guards.

Within just three days, students of all middle schools in that area rose up to establish their own Red Guard organizations. The oldest members were nineteen years old, the youngest only thirteen. The streets and alleys of Beijing now rang with the sound of children's voices shouting vitriolic slogans.

I witnessed the Red Guards' activities for the first time one day in June 1966.

Earlier that morning a pretty classmate named Yong Mei told me about the tensions between Tsinghua Middle School students and their school's administration.

The situation was this: the big-character poster that the Tsinghua Middle School students had put up on June 2 had been copied and posted on our own campus. Students at our school had immediately responded by forming an organization under the name "The Red Guards of Mao-Zedongism." The founding declaration was posted next to the copy of the Tsinghua Middle School students' poster. "We have to go show our support!" Yong Mei told me, then added, "Do you want to come along?"

Yong Mei came from a high-level PLA officer's family, and she initiated the Red Guards organization at my school. After listening to her rave about the Red Guards' bravery and idealism, I decided to tag along to a meeting with her. I didn't need to join the Red Guards organization quite yet—during the early days, becoming a member was quite simple as there was no paperwork to be filled in and no formalities of any kind. If you went along with whatever the Red Guards did, you were "in." You were one of them.

The next day I jumped onto the back seat of a classmate's bicycle and together we headed for Tsinghua Middle School. From a distance I saw dozens of students heading in the same direction. Nearly all of them, I noticed, came from high-level officials' families—mostly army officers from the Headquarters of the General Staff, the Navy, the Air Force, and the General Logistics Department. They wore army uniforms faded from years of wear and laundering, which lent the garments a forbidding authenticity.

Although I kept the observation to myself, I thought they looked quite smug with their rolled-up sleeves and thick army belts. I wasn't far from the mark. As far as these students were concerned, their parents' sacrifices and valor during the revolutionary war had bolstered the whole nation. To them, China was already theirs and they could do and say anything they pleased. "I will kill you!" became a catch phrase of the early Red Guards.

Nearly all the founding Red Guards hailed from the top three "categories" of society: families of army officers, government officials, or people who had died or were injured during revolutionary wars. Students whose parents were factory workers or peasants were, in theory, also qualified to join their ranks, but the "elite" comprised the majority, and members from workers' and peasants' families were in fact very few. As for the Red Guard leaders, without exception their family backgrounds fell within the first three categories.

When we arrived at Tsinghua Middle School, about two hundred students from other schools were already present and many more were on the way. The administration had closed the school gates to avoid any ugly incidents; supporters would have to wait outside. As I shouldered my way through the crowd, someone, possibly a school administrator, climbed onto a desk and began addressing the students. At first I couldn't hear what he was saying, but eventually I pushed my way to the front.

"Calm down!" he shouted. "Don't do anything impulsive, don't do anything the school hasn't already authorized. . ."

The warning only stoked the students' rage. One of them shouted, "Don't listen to him! Let's storm the campus!"

The students in the crowd fell into two groups, one that sided with the school administration, and the other against it. Those on the administration's side blocked the entrance to keep the supporters out. Students started pushing one another, and the situation quickly escalated.

All of a sudden a group of adults appeared. They separated the two sides before any more bodily contact could occur. The adults were plainclothes guards from the municipal Public Security Bureau, but I only learned that afterwards.

When neither side got the upper hand, someone produced a poetic couplet and posted it at the entrance. "Revolutionary pioneers have shed their blood for the revolution," read the verse on the left. "Their successors are willing to do anything to protect the country they established," read the one on the right. Many people cheered.

But there was a dissenting voice from a third-year student from Tsinghua High School. She came from a family of factory workers, which fell under the "five revolutionary categories." The big-character poster she wrote took the form of a letter addressed to the revolutionary "elite," those from families with government officials and army officers. "You are not Red Guards," she read in a loud, powerful voice. "You are black guards working for black organizations. The mountain behind you is not one of rocks, but an iceberg that may melt at any time." She ended with this rousing call, "We are shedding blood to protect the Party and the School Party Committee."

The applause she won was as strong as that for the opposite side. I was deeply confused. Who, I wondered, was right and who was wrong?

OUR TEACHERS, OUR ENEMIES

THERE'S A SEQUENCE OF IDOLS TRADITIONALLY WORSHIPPED IN Chinese culture that goes as follows: Heaven, Earth, the Sovereign, parents, and, finally, teachers. Throughout China's history, everyone from monarchs to peasants respected teachers and prized education. These values had prevailed for thousands of years, but the Cultural Revolution totally upended them.

With nearly all of the country's youth sporting Red Guard armbands, students now seemed determined to outdo their peers in terms of sheer insanity. Inspired by the creed "rebellion is always right," they dragged teachers to struggle sessions any time they felt like cursing, punching, kicking, cudgeling, or even whipping them. Teachers were simply not human; even killing them could be entirely justified. A historian would recount this telling episode from the early years of the Cultural Revolution:

> The Red Guards from Beijing Middle School
> Number Six [a school less than a mile from
> Tiananmen Tower] turned their music classroom
> into a makeshift prison. Guards and searchlights
> were seen on the roof night and day. The walls read,
> "Long Live the Red Terror." When these characters
> faded, the torturers repainted them in the blood of
> their victims.

Not only were teachers no longer venerated for their contributions to society; their very dignity as human beings was no more. Very few schools in China were left untouched by this radical ethical reversal; mine was not one of them.

Less than a year after I came to Beijing from Guangzhou, I enrolled in the Foreign Languages School in the Baiduizi district of Beijing. The area was home to a number of famous institutes of learning. Ours was a boarding school, with students returning home on Saturday and arriving back at school before Sunday evening. Every Saturday, I would walk to my parents' apartment on foot, passing broad stretches of fields and a couple of villages before arriving back home in Weigongcun.

It was a trek I gladly undertook. China was cut off from the outside world, with few diplomatic activities, and very few people spoke foreign languages. The Foreign Languages School was one of just two foreign-languages schools in Beijing. Described as a "cradle" for diplomats, it spanned primary school through high school. Six foreign languages were taught: English, French, Arabic, Spanish, Japanese, and German. It was indeed a school for the privileged. Many students came from high-ranking officials' families, the offspring of vice-ministers or vice-premiers. Admission was an honor, and I felt tremendously lucky to be accepted, especially since my father was not a high-ranking official. Due to the makeup of the student body, the Red Guards movement and their brutal campaign against teachers started earlier here than at other Beijing schools. What happened in June 1966 was nothing compared with later events of that summer. At first it was little more than the putting up of big-character posters, mostly in the auditorium and the students' canteen. The posters in the auditorium covered the walls from floor to ceiling, and in the canteen, not an inch of vacant space was left on walls both inside and outside. In terms of exchanging insider information, students from officials' families had more connections than most, and Red Guards from the middle schools affiliated with Tsinghua, Peking, and Renmin universities were busy copying big-character posters from one another. Printed pamphlets also helped news to spread. Many posters and pamphlets were meant to disclose the bourgeois lifestyle of some faculty members, including the school principal and dean of students, calling them out for things like fancy, Western-style wardrobes. Some early posters targeted foreign teachers from the UK, France, Japan, and Cuba, who had come to teach at the government's invitation.

These big-character posters manifested a unique style of language never seen before or (possibly) afterward. Every passage exuded hatred. The posters always began with a quotation from Chairman Mao Zedong, something like: "A revolution is not a dinner party, or writing an essay, or painting a picture, or doing embroidery; it cannot be so refined, so leisurely and gentle, so temperate, kind, courteous, restrained, and magnanimous. A revolution is an insurrection, an act of violence by which one class overthrows another." Or the ever-popular line: "Of all the principles of Marxism, the basic one is this: Rebellion is always right!"

By mid-June of 1966, the school had stopped functioning. Were we going to take exams as usual, or would the summer vacation continue indefinitely? No one knew. The administration had been dismantled. Meanwhile, a spirit of rebellion took over the student body. Some Red Guards rushed to the middle schools affiliated with Peking and Tsinghua Universities, their two "holy" sites, to learn and return with novel tricks on how to torture teachers more effectively—for example, dunce-capping them, hanging a plaque around their necks, and slapping them in the face during struggle sessions.

This made me uncomfortable. Was I right to feel that way? I put this question to Father one weekend. His words etched themselves in my mind: "Your mother is a teacher," he began. "If somebody did that to her, would you be happy?"

Father had survived the anti-rightist movement of 1957. After it was over, he repeatedly admonished me and my older brother: "Never stand against your school's Party committee or the working team sent by the government. Be cautious, always!" The trick applied during that movement was old but effective: They would encourage you to say anything on your mind first, and then label you a "rightist" and denounce you. By the time you found out what had happened, your fate was sealed.

"Never," Father said with emphasis, "fall victim to that trick and be called a juvenile rightist!" Other things he taught me were equally unforgettable: "Don't let anyone use you" and "Never take a fall like that, because you are still young and you have a long way to go in life."

A working team from the Beijing Municipal Government arrived in early June, seizing control of my school. According to the team, in the realm of education, revolution should never be conducted violently, and no teachers should be humiliated. The Red Guard movement cooled down, and for a period of time—in July, in particular—peace returned to campus. Most students supported the team. To them, the team had been sent by the Party and we should therefore follow their directions. But not all students thought this way; those from high-ranking officials' families were notably of a different mind.

A major shift took place in late July, when the Party Central Committee set up a leading group for the Cultural Revolution. Madame Mao's stance was unequivocal: "Students," she said, "should rise in rebellion against the working teams from the government." For a brief time, rebellion was sporadic, but then, after July 18 when Mao Zedong received the Red Guards for the first time in Tiananmen Square, violence engulfed campuses. With Chairman Mao's benediction and tacit permission from other higher-ups, the Red Guards turned downright brutal. The more savage they became, the more violence they applied, the more revolutionary they considered themselves.

The Red Guards at my school now escalated their activities. One struggle session was held in the dormitory building for male students. The targets included Principal Mo Ping, Party Committee Secretary Cheng Bi, Vice-Principal Lei Li, Dean of Students Yao Shuxi, and her assistant, Zhang Chengjiu. Each of them was dunce-capped, a plaque hung on their chests with their names written in black but crossed out with red ink. Cheng Bi and Yao Shuxi were female. To humiliate them, the Red Guards shaved off half their hair, a very popular practice when punishing women. Desks were configured to create makeshift stands. The teachers were made to kneel on top of them, heads low in the middle of the four legs of a chair placed upside down in front of each of them. This was just one of the torture techniques; there were many others.

I had interacted with all but one of the targets, Cheng Bi. Yao Shuxi and Zhang Chengjiu left very good impressions on me the first time we met. One day, when I was just starting school there, Mother took me to campus to finish up some paperwork. Yao Shuxi and Zhang Chengjiu were there to receive us. Father was just one of the many who worked for the government—not a high-ranking person at all, and we had no reason to expect special treatment.

I'd had a medical checkup before I left Guangzhou, and my blood pressure had shot up to 140, probably from nervousness. Yao Shuxi hesitated when he saw my medical report. Mother was uncertain how to explain the problem. Zhang Chengjiu, whom we had just met, stepped in and helped out from the sidelines. "Even I have a minor problem with blood pressure," he said with a smile. What he said put an end to the awkwardness. After scrutinizing my placement scores, Yao Shuxi put me in the advanced class. When Father found out about this later that day, he was quite pleased, especially when Mother explained the kind treatment we'd received.

These two were now among the people to be publicly humiliated. I couldn't show it, but I was sad and also confused about what happened to them. All the perpetrators were teenagers, mostly male, a few female. Compared to the boys, the girls seemed exceptionally excited. I remember a certain bespectacled girl. In my memory, no struggle session on campus was ever conducted without her, and she always chaired the proceedings with a cold, ruthless air.

As was routine, the struggle session began with the song *The East Is Red*:

> The east is red, the sun rises.
> China has brought forth a Mao Zedong.
> He amasses fortune for the people, Hurrah,
> He is the people's liberating star....

The session closed with another, no less revolutionary ballad, *Sailing the Seas Depends on the Helmsman*, which went like this:

> Sailing the seas depends on the helmsman,
> Life and growth depends on the sun.
> Rain and dew drops nourish the crops,
> Undertaking revolution depends on Mao Zedong's thought!

The night of that struggle session, I was unable to fall asleep. The moment I closed my eyes, disturbing images drifted into my mind, and I couldn't shake them loose no matter how hard I tried.

On the instruction of the leading group for the Cultural Revolution, the working team sent by the Beijing Municipal Government withdrew, yielding its place to the students.

To the young and energetic Red Guards, without exception all faculty members were bad and deserved to be tossed into the garbage can of history. Some of these "bad people" were actually imprisoned inside the classrooms where they had once taught. For a period of time, they were made to line up every day at the entrance to the students' canteen, heads bent low and stooped down at the waist, where they were laughed at and scorned by students on their way to taking their meals. The teachers had plaques hanging from their necks. Whenever a student walked by, they were instructed to say loudly, "We're devils, devils, devils. . ."

Occasionally, they were made to sing—no, to howl—a song especially composed for them. It went:

> I'm bad, I'm the people's enemy.
> I have committed a crime and I deserve to die.
> Please smash me, smash me.
> I'm bad.
>
> I must plead guilty.
> I need to reform,
> I need to change,
> Or I will surely die.

A Red Guard from Beijing Middle School Number 4 wrote the lyrics, but the music had been composed by Zhou Weizhi, the composer of *The Song of Chinese People's Volunteers*. Zhou Weizhi would serve as Minister of Culture after the Cultural Revolution. At the time, however, he was himself one of the "bad people." The Red Guards made use of him, ordering him to compose the score for this humiliating song. If teachers were ever out of tune or missed a beat, punches and kicks rained down on them.

Some Red Guards at school now slapped teachers in the face at any time they felt like it, and no resistance or tears were allowed. Most of these teachers were not young, and standing for a dozen hours a day was both a physical and mental torture. But in order to survive, they had to endure it. There was no choice.

Every time I walked into the canteen, my heart dropped at the sight of the teachers who'd been singled out for punishment, especially the female teachers whose hair had been shaved off. I just didn't know how to help them, or if I even *should* help. Were they really guilty? Not only did I not know what to make of what was happening at school, I questioned whether I should even allow myself to dwell on such questions.

THE MONKEY KINGS

BY JUNE 1966, THE RED GUARD MOVEMENT WAS RAMPANT—nearly a million strong and rapidly growing. In an effort to keep it under control, a working team from the Beijing Municipal Government was sent to Tsinghua Middle School. The team lost no time denouncing the Red Guards as counterrevolutionary.

This announcement was met with considerable resistance, as was seen on another big-character poster by the Red Guards entitled "Long Live the Proletarian and Revolutionary Spirit of Revolt." The working team was infuriated. "The Communist Party of China is the ruling party," they insisted. "Who are you against?" The Red Guards of the school retorted by quoting Chairman Mao: "To rise in rebellion is, after all, the ultimate truth of Marxism." With both sides locked into their respective points of view, the situation rapidly became explosive.

Some friends from the Middle School of Peking University

invited me to a July 1 party to celebrate the forty-five year anniversary of the Chinese Communist Party. The organizers showed their open displeasure toward the university's working team and dissenting student groups with much fanfare. Beautiful invitation cards were printed, and all the guests invited were from Party or Government officials' families. They even had a dress code—army uniform only.

Dozens of students from my school attended the event. I didn't have an army uniform to wear to the party, but I hoped that somehow I would get in anyway.

The party took place on the Tsinghua Middle School campus, in a Russian-style building—red in color and very tall in the middle with wings flanking both sides. The festivities were held toward the front of the building and the roof of the boiler room to the side had been fashioned into a temporary stage, with searchlights set up all around it to light up the evening sky. There was even a student orchestra at the ready.

My school had an orchestra, too, but it couldn't compare with this one—we had no more than a couple of flutes and Chinese *huqin* violins. When I arrived, the orchestra was playing a very happy melody, "The Chinese New Year is Here," a very popular dance in the northern Shaanxi at the time Mao and the Party Central Committee formed their revolutionary base there. The lively music heightened the atmosphere. On the other side of the venue, people were dancing *yangge* to the tune.

When that song ended, the band struck up one I didn't recognize. The music and lyrics of this song had been composed by students just that afternoon. It was called "The

Song of Rebellion" and everyone committed it to memory before too long. The song had a pleasant melody, but the lyrics were chilling:

> Our writing brushes are weapons against the
> reactionary gang
> Revolutionary people rise in rebellion, faculty
> members and students alike;
>
> We are revolutionary fighters of the Cultural
> Revolution,
> Loyal to the Party and the Revolutionary cause;
>
> The Party is our mother
> We will kill anyone who is against her—kill, kill
> and kill!

I was mulling over this new song when one of my classmates pointed out the founders of the Red Guards, the famous Bu Dahua among them. We shouldered our way through the crowd to get within hearing distance. Bu Dahua and the others were excitedly telling admirers from other schools how they had founded the Red Guards at the ruins of the Old Summer Palace. They were all dressed in faded army uniforms. With the addition of army caps and belts, each of them cut an impressive figure.

The parents of these Red Guards were all high-ranking officials; as the older generation struggled to seize state power, their children cultivated a deep sense of superiority. About twenty days later, some Red Guards would post an astonishing poetic couplet—its left side read, "Heroes come only from the families of high-ranking officials," and the right side read, "The children of counterrevolutionary families are bastards!" The horizontal message between each side further stressed the point: "No exceptions!"

Peng Xiaomeng, a very good speaker and the leader of the Red Guards at the Middle School of Peking University, chaired the gathering. Later, when Chairman Mao greeted the Red Guards in Tiananmen Square, she was one of those chosen to make a speech.

But on this evening, someone from Tsinghua Middle School impressed me more than anybody else. I would forget his name, but what he said is still etched into my mind. Microphone in hand, he began to read a big-character poster he had brushed just seven days beforehand:

> Revolution is to rebel after all. Such is the soul of Mao Thought. When we say 'implement Mao Thought,' we mean to rebel: dare to say, think, do, pioneer, and perform revolutionary activities. In short, to rebel, and this is the most precious quality of a proletarian revolutionary. It is the fundamental principle of proletarian Party awareness. Refuse to rebel? You are absolutely a revisionist.

> Revisionists have controlled our schools for seventeen years. The time is now or never to rebel! Some of the antagonists are timid today, mumbling things like 'one-sidedness, arrogance, violence, too much,' and so on and so forth. Nonsense! If you

oppose something, do it openly. It is not up to you
if we rise and rebel. We will use bullets, explosives,
hand grenades and blasting cartridges, anything we
can lay our hands on in fighting revisionists. 'Human
feelings?' 'Thoughtfulness?' To Hell! You have
blamed us as 'one-sided.' But look at what you did.
'Combining two into one?' This is utter eclecticism.

Are we too arrogant for you? Well yes, that's exactly
what we want. Chairman Mao said, 'We counted the
mighty as no better than muck!' We are determined
to overthrow not only the counterrevolutionaries of
the school, but throughout the world. When we have
the world in mind, how can we accomplish that
mission without being 'arrogant'?

You said we were brutal. Yes, you are right! How
can we be nice and gentle to revisionism? That is
brutality to the revolution.

You said that we have gone too far. You are right
again! It will be reformism or peaceful transition if
we do not! Think twice if that's what you want! We
are going to knock you over and put our foot firmly
down upon your body!

You are scared of revolution and rebellion. You are
all 'yes men,' observing rules and regulations. You
take shelter in a snail shell and your nerves jump
whenever a wind rises. Over the past few weeks, you

have heard bad news every day. You are about to break down! How can you stand being so nervous, day after day?

Revolutionaries are like the Monkey King. His golden cudgel is mighty and merciless. He has a far-reaching supernatural power capable of sweeping all of you off your horses. Your world will be turned upside down, inside out. The golden cudgel is none other than the invincible Mao Thought, which we are going to use against the old world of yours, to shred it to pieces. We must destroy this revisionist Tsinghua Middle School. We won't stop until it falls apart. Like the Monkey King, we are going to fight all the way up to Heaven, for the birth of a brand new proletarian world on Earth.

That summer, as the Red Guards swelled with new members, The Great Leader decided to go for a swim.

Chairman Mao harbored no doubts about the esteem he enjoyed among the masses, and he was an expert in making use of their strength to augment his own. This time, he believed he could mobilize people against his opponents. For him, the stakes were very high. Mao considered the Cultural Revolution his greatest legacy. "I have done just two things," he once said about his life. "The first was to fight Chiang Kai-shek for decades until I drove him to a couple of small islands, fighting Japanese aggression for eight years until they went back home and I was in the Forbidden City of Beijing; the second, starting this Cultural Revolution." What he meant was this: He fought for China's national interest and sovereignty and then he fought to preserve it.

But Mao was now seventy-three years old. Even if he possessed a will of iron, did he have sufficient strength to guard his legacy?

He seemed uncharacteristically worried that summer. Everybody knew that he loved swimming and that he'd swum in the Yangtze River several times. On July 16, he did it again. Setting out from the dam in Wuchang, it reportedly took him just one hour and five minutes to cover a distance of nearly ten miles. Swimming at such a speed was an astonishing feat at any age, and if true, Mao achieved a world-record pace that day.

On July 25, news of Mao's swim hit the front pages of China's newspapers with the title "The Most Excellent News." This immediately gave rise to a nationwide campaign "to wish Chairman Mao a long life." Privately, some people saw the swimming story as a form of propaganda no different from the exaggerations of China's former imperial elite. Some took it as a publicity stunt to win votes, as politicians in the West did every day. Still others saw another possibility: Mao needed to be sure of his physical prowess at his advanced age, when there was some doubt as to whether he had enough energy left to go to war against his powerful opponents and to safeguard his political beliefs.

Nobody knew for sure what Mao intended, but by swimming in the Yangtze, Mao signaled confidence in his physical condition and, by extension, confidence that he could win yet another political battle. The swim was also a touchstone for the personality cult he enjoyed among the masses. People's reactions to the news showed that his popularity had not diminished in the least.

MADAME MAO'S HAT

THE FIRST TIME I SAW MADAME MAO SHE WAS WEARING A GREEN army cap.

Madame Mao, or Jiang Qin as she was known in China, lived a life riddled with drama. A strikingly beautiful woman and one-time actress, she married Mao in 1938, when she was twenty-four years old and he was forty-five. Until 1966 she lingered at the periphery of the country's political scene, but during the Cultural Revolution she quickly rose to great prominence. The highest leader of the Cultural Revolution leading group, Madame Mao was also a member of the Political Bureau of the ninth and tenth Party Central Committees.

Her fate would prove especially cruel. A few weeks after Mao's death in 1976, Madame Mao was arrested and imprisoned. She was sentenced to death in 1981, but her punishment was later changed to life imprisonment. On May 14, 1991, while on medical parole, Madame Mao, the "white-boned demon," committed suicide by hanging herself.

But during the "Ten Thousand People's Debate" of July 25-26, 1966, Madame Mao was still very much alive. On a hot and suffocating summer evening, she entered the fray, laying bare the conflicts raging within the CCP Central Committee. Her appearance there was part of her broader tactic of inciting the Red Guards to revolt against other senior political leaders and government officials.

And if there was any doubt, the green army cap on her head made it clear: this was war.

Her first, and in some respects most chilling, campaign was waged against Wang Guangmei, the wife of President Liu Shaoqi.

Wang Guangmei served as the vice director of the working team sent to Tsinghua University. She and her fellow workers had a very difficult time with the task. A student leader by the name of Kuai Dafu demanded a public debate with the first lady's team. He even called on his fellow students to revolt and to seize control of the university.

For Wang Guangmei and her colleagues, this went too far. Such a blatant reactionary act should never be tolerated. Kuai Dafu was kicked out of the Youth League and then jailed. Kuai Dafu protested with a hunger strike. Wang Guangmei and her fellow workers didn't know what to do next.

At that time, each university had a working team from the government. For them, the situation had turned dire. Take Peking University, for instance. After so many people were publicly humiliated and physically attacked, the government's working team at the university showed zero tolerance by labeling every student involved a "right-winger."

Students split into two distinct parties. Those supporting the working team believed nobody had the right to engage in violence and personal insults. The other side opposed everything the team had done thus far. They tried to justify the events of June 18th by invoking Mao's words in *Report on an Investigation of the Peasant Movement in Hunan*: "A revolution is not a dinner party, or writing an essay, or painting a picture, or doing embroidery. . .it is an insurrection, an act of violence by which one class overthrows another."

Both sides believed they were revolutionary and the other side not. As the feud intensified, big-character posters sprang up everywhere, papering every surface of the university's campus.

"Who do you think it will be?" my friend asked as we peered at the empty stage.

I'd gone to Tsinghua University with two classmates to see what was happening there first-hand. We wanted to know if Kuai Dafu had really been jailed. After walking around campus for a while, we were thinking about going home when we heard the news: Someone from the Cultural Revolution's leading group would be appearing for the "Ten Thousand People's Debate."

Our interest was immediately kindled. With a couple of steamed buns each to kill our hunger, we snuck into the meeting through Peking University's eastern gate.

The sky was already dark when we reached the sporting grounds. There were no stars in the sky, but the area was well-lit. Peking University students streamed into the grounds, marching in formation. Before long, the arena was completely full. My classmates and I were just spectators, moving from one spot to another for a better view. The debate, people said, would start at eight that evening. But the seats on the stage were still empty. People became even more expectant; a delay usually meant the arrival of an important person.

So far the Peking University students were behaving themselves—much to my surprise. They stayed in the area that had been designated to them. Nobody was wandering around. They just sang one revolutionary song after another.

Why are they so patient? I wondered.

Later, I came to know the answer. The topics of the night's debate were too symbolic for them to make trouble: "Was the June 18th Incident Revolutionary or Anti-Revolutionary?" and "Did the Work Team Handle the Incident Correctly?" The outcome of the debate would affect the fate of everyone, teachers and students alike. Even the CCP Central Committee was keenly interested in the outcome, as evinced by the many high-ranking officials in attendance.

The rostrum was about a hundred meters wide with several rows of seats. Even so, the seating was insufficient and some of the officials had to stand.

Chen Boda, a key figure in the Cultural Revolution, chaired the debate. It began with speeches by people from this group, then student representatives from each side spoke. Both groups presented strong arguments; both sides quoted Chairman Mao to justify themselves and to prove the other was wrong.

Suddenly the sky cracked open and rain began to fall. If not for the downpour, the debate would have likely gone on forever. People had no choice but to resume the debate the next day.

★★★

The sight of Madame Mao in a green army cap would always be among the most memorable moments from that event. "Comrades," she began, "Chairman Mao sent us to learn from you, to be students on the revolutionary side. We will also come whenever faculty members of the university need us. If you believe we have made a mistake, you may write a big-character poster, or write to Chairman Mao directly, or go and see him. We work for the revolutionary side. The revolutionaries may go with us, while those against revolution may leave. You have different ideas, I know. You can speak and we want to listen."

When she finished her speech, she returned to her chair. But then, when Kang Sheng had the floor, she suddenly rose and made her way to the microphone. She shoved Kang Sheng aside and shouted something to the effect of, "I have come to argue against the wife of Mao Anqing [Mao's second-born son]! Her mother is a liar! She had sex with Mao Anqing when he was in a confused state of mind. She cheated him into marriage!"

It was an extraordinary moment. The first family's dirty laundry had just been aired publicly—and on such a grave occasion. Feng Xuefeng would recount the event in his memoirs:

> At about 11 p.m. [Madame Mao] rose to speak. "I have been to Peking University four times," she said. Then she suddenly changed the subject by saying, "Class struggle has come into my home. Espionage from the enemy has come to my home. Is Zhang Shaohua here? Let's see what kind of people Zhang Chengxian has used. Zhang Shaohua is in the leading group. Her mother, Zhang Wenqiu, is a notorious political swindler. Zhang Shaohua is self-styled as the daughter-in-law of Chairman Mao, but none of us has acknowledged it." [Madame Mao] broke into tears. "This is a class struggle taking place in my own home. I didn't have a heart problem before, but now, I do. I want to disclose their actions!"

"Not here," Chen Boda reportedly whispered to her. At this, Madame Mao lowered her voice and said, "I have endured this woman and her family for a decade. They are like stones in my shoes!"

She clearly didn't expect that their whispers would be broadcast over the loudspeakers. Even though I only vaguely understood what she'd said, I found the episode intensely embarrassing.

But I was in for much more.

Peng Xiaomeng took the stage. Xiaomeng's father was then the vice chairman of the China Red Cross, and her mother a writer. She was only seventeen at the time, a student at the middle school affiliated with Peking University. She spoke as a representative of the Red Guard. She was obviously a good speaker, and what she said was quite passionate.

A month earlier, she'd written this on a big-character poster: "We are the repudiators of the old society and protectors and builders of the new one. The task before us is difficult. I have been at school for ten years. I have heard numerous capitalist and revisionist ideas on campus." Her poster went on to state:

> Some people have styled themselves as 'gardeners,' but what they have tried to do is to cut off fresh buds. Some wear a smile all the time. They look gentle and morally upright, but actually they are people of the school of Confucius, thieves and hooligans. So far, no country in the world has developed a new education system for the proletariat. We are here to take on the task. With the care and leadership of Chairman Mao and the Party Central Committee, we are confident in accomplishing that mission. We are capable of doing it. We won't let the Party Central Committee and Chairman Mao down. We will go on forever as fearless fighters in this proletarian Cultural Revolution.

That day her fearlessness was fully manifest. At the time, Zhang Chengxian was the leader of the working team sent to Peking University. He was the one to bear the brunt when

Peng Xiaomeng accused the working team of the persecution she claimed to have suffered. Kang Sheng added much fuel from the side by saying, "Zhang Chengxian is more than a reactionary; he is also anti-Party, anti-socialist, and a counter-reactionary!"

What happened next shocked me. Peng Xiaomeng slipped her belt loose and began whipping Zhang Chengxian with it. Several Red Guards on the rostrum joined her. Madame Mao, Kang Sheng, and Chen Boda did not try to stop them. The beating occurred right before the eyes of thousands.

How, I asked myself, could that pretty, normal-looking girl act so viciously? There was only one explanation I could think of: She was driven by earnest belief.

It didn't matter who won the debate, as would later be revealed. The Cultural Revolution's head group had come up with a conclusion of its own. What mattered was this: The conflict in the Party Central Committee had been made public. Before the meeting drew to a close, the group declared its decision to withdraw the working team from Peking University. They'd become an obstacle in the way of the revolutionary movement, and now they had to go.

★★★

Ten days later, Mao and Liu Shaoqi, the State President, clashed for the first time—the only open clash until then in their decades of cooperation. It happened at a small meeting of the Party Central Committee when Mao accused Liu Shaoqi of "being afraid of the masses."

"I have held my head high for decades doing revolutionary work," Liu Shaoqi reportedly argued. "How can I be afraid of the masses?"

"Your working teams," Mao said, "were sent to suppress their movements. It's a dictatorship."

"Dictatorship?" Liu Shaoqi retorted. "Far from it. It was a decision made by the Central Committee." He pressed ahead, saying, "The worst thing for me is to step down, and I'm not afraid of it."

The next day, Mao wrote *Bombard the General Head-quarters—My Big-Character Poster*. It was circulated first inside the Party. I came to know of it a year later, when it was published in the *People's Daily*. In this piece, Mao once again praised Nie Yuanzi's big-character poster, describing it as "the first poster of Marxism across the country."

"Over the past fifty-odd days," Mao wrote, "many leading officials on different levels have acted against the Cultural Revolution by suppressing the revolutionary people. They held a capitalist dictatorship from a capitalist position. What they have done is to commit sabotage and to call black white. They are very arrogant. They have suppressed different ideas by 'white terror.' They are on the capitalist side acting against the proletariat. How vicious they are!" Even though Liu Shaoqi's name was not mentioned, everybody knew that Mao was referring to him.

At the end of July, the Red Guards of Tsinghua Middle School astounded the nation with another big-character poster, *On the Revolutionary Spirit of Rebellion Once Again*. As before, it quoted Chairman Mao: "Of all the principles in Marxism, rebellion is the ultimate truth. By it, we should rise in rebellion, to fight and to construct socialism." More than any other quotation by Mao, this would be invoked constantly by Red Guards throughout the Cultural Revolution.

The authorities, however, were furious at this turn of events. The harsh measures they adopted had failed. The Red Guards had resisted strongly. How did they manage to summon such unusual courage? I probed my mind for an answer, but didn't find any. All I could think was that the students from high-ranking official families had been tipped off by their parents, and they knew they would prevail.

Facing enormous pressure, the Red Guards began to turn elsewhere for support. Once again, it was the Red Guards of Tsinghua Middle School who led the way. On July 28, they sent copies of the two big-character posters they had written, together with a letter, to Madame Mao. They asked her to pass them on to her husband. "Some people have taken our posters as reactionary," they entreated. "Please take a look to see if they are right."

Madame Mao didn't let them down. She showed the letter to Mao, who wrote back to the Red Guards just a few days later. In his letter he expressed his "warm support." "My revolutionary colleagues and I are firmly on your side," Mao wrote. "We support anyone in Beijing and across the country who thinks likewise during the Cultural Revolution."

Their letter and the big-character poster Mao wrote on August 5 were not published at the time. Still, the words winged their way across Beijing, and from there began to shake the entire country. The Red Guards' platform within the Cultural Revolution was now a given, and they would not be stopped.

Between August and November 1966, over a series of eight occasions, Chairman Mao greeted more than 10 million Red Guards and students in Beijing.

Waving their *Little Red Books*, students and their teachers salute Mao Zedong on the Tiananmen Rostrum.

The "Red Ocean" (hong haiyang) of the Cultural Revolution, consisting of red flags, red posters, red books, and the red sun, which symbolized Mao, filled Tiananmen Square and the surrounding streets in Beijing.

THE GREATEST RALLY IN HISTORY

Now it was August 1966.

The streets around Tiananmen Square were like rivers, the crowds like torrential waves. Just after sunset I boarded a truck heading for the square along with other students from my school. About a hundred of us were crammed into trucks and buses and driven caravan-style through the streets of Beijing.

I still didn't feel quite at home in my new life yet, but here, suddenly, was my chance to belong.

My blood surged as Tiananmen Square came into sight. Traveling by foot and by truck, thousands of young students flooded the streets from all directions, holding their red flags and placards high in the air. Some wore faded green army jackets and caps and bright-red armbands, designating their Red Guard status. As they marched through the city, people belted out revolutionary songs. Excitement was written on every face.

Having met secretly at the Old Summer Palace in May, the Red Guards seized Mao's endorsement and burst onto the revolutionary scene. They were nothing like American Scouts or even other youth organizations in China's other major city, Hong Kong; not only did the Red Guards revolt against anything old and established, they were willing to shed blood and even to die for the revolution.

On August 18, 1966, the nearly one million students and Red Guards weren't heading out to revolt, but to celebrate. Chairman Mao himself had summoned us to Tiananmen Square to rally for the "Proletariat Cultural Revolution." Vast crowds were expected, and because it was impossible to coordinate a single meeting time, many groups headed out for the square a whole night in advance.

That night, the many hundreds of thousands of voices seemed loud enough to rip open the pitch-dark sky. I was fourteen years old and my voice was among them.

✳✳✳

It was an unusually crisp summer night. I was wearing only a thin, short-sleeved shirt and a pair of slacks. I'd come from the south, where the weather was hot and humid, and I was totally unused to Beijing's cold, but that was the least of my troubles.

I was still struggling to fit in at school. My Mandarin was far from perfect, or even satisfactory. Whenever I opened my mouth, the other students laughed at my strong southern accent. I was also still short and skinny for my age. This had never worried me back in Guangdong, but in Beijing my appearance made me self-conscious. The other students all seemed taller and better-looking than I was. When we stood in formation, I was always directed toward the end of the line, behind the other boys and girls, and my cheeks burned with humiliation.

And then there was another problem: my clothes. As members of the educated class, neither of my parents was especially particular about clothing, but that wasn't the source of the trouble. Daily necessities were strictly rationed, and you needed coupons to buy anything—including clothes. Because there were five people in my family, our clothing coupons were spread very thin. In fact, this had become one of my parents' biggest headaches. What if we kids grew up too fast? How would they manage to clothe us?

My parents purposely bought us clothing several sizes too big for us; that way they'd be ready and waiting for us to grow into them. The pants we wore, for instance, were baggy in the crotch and so long in the legs that we had to roll them up three times at the hem. It was embarrassing to walk around with these ill-fitting clothes, but there was nothing at all I could do about it.

This might not have been so bad except that the school I attended, the Beijing Foreign Languages School, enrolled many students from Beijing's most elite families. Surrounded by the sons and daughters of government ministers and other high-ranking figures, I'd developed a serious inferiority complex. The seniors at school were already quite physically developed, and to me they looked very smug in their fashionable army uniforms and boots.

I, of course, had none of these desirable items. Back in Guangdong I'd walked around barefoot like everyone else. I now wore a pair of traditional cloth shoes that my parents bought for me soon after we moved to Beijing, but these shoes were a far cry from the military-style boots my classmates favored.

In addition to their good looks and impressive clothes, my classmates all had two things in common: the goal of becoming government leaders and the conviction that they would succeed. My own ambitions were less defined. From my father I'd picked up a love of books and history, but I lacked the confidence that seemed to come so naturally to the others at my school.

Still, I wouldn't have given up the chance to be at this school for anything. Beijing wasn't just the capital of China, it was the center of the world—or so it seemed to me back then. At the Beijing Foreign Languages School I felt privy to all the most interesting and important issues of the day. The halls and classrooms teemed with whispers and rumors about the government's inner workings.

In fact, just that week I'd heard that factions inside the Party and government were conspiring against Chairman Mao. When I heard the rumor, I thought, a conspiracy against Mao? It was a shocking and unthinkable prospect.

Like my classmates, I was ready to fight—and at any cost—for Mao. Waiting outside the gates of Tiananmen Square that August 1966 night, I kept reminding myself that we were all revolutionaries, and that meant we were comrades. Besides, a true revolutionary should never feel inferior on account of such a superficial matter as clothing.

That's a pathetic bourgeois sentiment, I scolded myself, rubbing my arms to warm myself from the cold.

"Do you think Chairman Mao is around here somewhere?" I asked a girl sitting next to me on the bus. Her eyebrows arched. "I suppose it's possible," she said before quickly turning her face back to the window.

The bus was still parked on a street west of the Tiananmen Rostrum. We'd been instructed to stay there until further notice.

The wait felt interminable.

I peered out the window. From my vantage point, I could see huge numbers of people on their way to Tiananmen Square. They were all shouting, singing, holding red flags and posters emblazoned with revolutionary slogans.

Was it really possible we'd encounter Mao tonight? Chairman Mao lived in Zhongnanhai—everyone knew that. Zhongnanhai had once been a royal garden, and it was now technically part of the Forbidden City. The character "hai" in its name meant "sea" in Chinese, although it was only a lake, not a sea, that graced the property. After the founding of the New China, a street was built to separate Zhongnanhai from the Forbidden City. The latter became a world-famous tourist attraction, while the former became the Communist Party headquarters. Mao's private residence was situated directly inside the complex.

At this moment, our truck was parked right outside that compound. There was now just a wall between me and Chairman Mao. It was a thrilling thought.

Even though I was just fourteen years old, I'd long since been primed to idolize Mao. Beginning in kindergarten, my mind, like all members of my generation, had been stuffed full of ideology. "There would be no New China without the Communist Party," I'd been taught since earliest childhood. A popular song from those times described him as "the red sun in our heart." "Mao is the nation's great savior" was another phrase emblazoned in my brain.

To me—and nearly all Chinese of that era—Mao was quite simply a god.

Waiting outside the CCP headquarters, I couldn't believe I was so close to my god and the red sun in my heart. *Please,* I thought to myself, *let a miracle occur. Let me pass through the wall to see Chairman Mao. Let me get just one look at him, even from a distance!*

Of course, I was unable to pass through the wall. Even so, I felt a warmth pass through me on that cold night as I entertained this fantasy. When I looked around, I sensed that all of the other students felt the same. We were bound together by our faith, longing, and hope.

At two o'clock in the morning, a whistle finally sounded. Soldiers appeared to announce the rules, and then we formed a line and set out again. It was totally dark; the sky above was starless. The soldiers led us into Zhongshan Park through its west gate. "One, two, three, four!" they shouted, and we proceeded in precise order. *We must look like we're soldiers, too,* I thought. In the darkness, we started singing an old military anthem. "Let's do combat, let's do combat, we have bayoneted rifles and grenades in hand—"

Startled birds took wing from the treetops as we approached the cypress woods. "Wait here!" a soldier shouted. I was worried we'd have to wait a long time, but it wasn't long before we lined up to move ahead again. From the park's eastern exit, we stepped up the viewing stands on the west side of Tiananmen Tower. This was my first time visiting Tiananmen Square and I was completely overwhelmed by what I saw. Tiananmen Square drew its name—the Gate of Heavenly Peace—from the massive stone situated near what had once been the main gate to the Forbidden City. Built in 1651, the square was enlarged to four times its original size in 1958, covering an area of one hundred acres. To facilitate assemblies and parades—of which there would be many during the Cultural Revolution—every single flagstone in the square bore a number.

I knew that Tiananmen was the biggest city square in the world, yet my first view of it completely shocked me. In later years, I'd visit other famous city squares around the world: the National Mall in Washington, D.C., Trafalgar Square in London, the Place de la Concorde in Paris, the Roman Forum in Frankfurt—but none would seem as spectacular as Tiananmen Square, not even close.

It wasn't just the enormity of the square that overtook me, but the sea of red flags and posters crowding it. The most eye-catching was a giant rectangular model placed at the very center of the square. It bore the famous large-character poster by Nie Yuanzi, the philosophy lecturer at Peking University. Chairman Mao had described it as "the first-ranking revolutionary large-character poster." Students from Peking University were granted a special favor because of it: They were permitted to surround the poster. Thousands of students from all over the country fanned out from this point, reaching out in all directions.

More than anything, the sheer number of faces stunned me. There wasn't an inch of space left in Tiananmen Square. Many people had also gathered along nearby Chang'an Avenue, desperate for a glimpse of the spectacle. Wherever I looked, all I could see were people—and more people. The next day, when I read about the event in the newspaper, I learned that more than a million people had come together in that huge, but still limited space. There had never been a rally on this scale anywhere in the world, and I had been a part of it.

As bodies pressed in on me from every side, I closed my eyes and imagined myself riding in a helicopter and looking down at Tiananmen Square. In my mind's eye I saw a gigantic cross made up of red flags, red armbands, and a million black-haired human heads.

It was August 18, 1966. The darkest hour of night was dawning, and soon Mao would appear.

THE RED SUN
IN OUR HEARTS

ANYONE PASSNG THROUGH BEIJING THAT AUGUST NIGHT MIGHT have thought the city was celebrating a carnival. In fact, that date saw one of the worst catastrophes in human history.

Chairman Mao mounted the Tiananmen Rostrum at sunrise. After he ascended the tower by elevator, Mao veered away from the evening's script and made a snap decision: He would enter among the masses. Nobody could say no to him. Flanked by his personnel, he stepped down from the tower to Gold Water Bridge and appeared suddenly from within the crowd.

There was a moment of shocked silence, followed by raucous cheers. Tears streamed down seemingly every face. People burst out, "Long Live Chairman Mao!" The song "The East is Red" boomed from every loudspeaker in the square. "Long Live Chairman Mao!" people shouted thunderously yet again.

I was beside myself with excitement. Gold Water Bridge

was just a hundred meters from where I stood, but I was short and all I could see was a forest of raised arms, many waving the *Little Red Book*. I did the same, shouting "Long Live Chairman Mao!" at the top of my lungs.

I stood on my toes; my eyes were searching everywhere for Mao.

And then it happened: I saw him.

Chairman Mao's face appeared at the center of the crowd on Gold Water Bridge. He flashed in and out of my field of vision. Time slowed down and seemed to stop altogether. I was dizzy with excitement. Until this day I had only seen pictures of him, but now he was here in the flesh.

"Long Live Chairman Mao!" I cried out as tears streamed down my face. I shouted so hard and for so long that my voice went hoarse. I thought that if I shouted loud enough he would hear me, recognizing me among the thousands of others.

At that very moment, the sun began to rise in the east from the end of Chang'an Avenue, bathing everything and everyone below in red. My vision and my imagination merged. I witnessed a miracle: Mao was ascending from the bridge to the sky in rays of golden light. He was smiling at me, he was waving at me. It wasn't an illusion; at that moment, it was completely real to me. I'd left my body behind, and only my ecstatic soul was left.

When I next caught sight of him, Mao was smiling broadly, his face aglow. As he crossed Gold Water Bridge, he shook hands with the students from Peking University. His hands seemed to have a magical power. Every hand he took into his own trembled with ecstasy, which then registered immediately on that person's face. Later, a Peking University student would recall: "From that moment on, I was determined to do anything for him—even to die!"

"Why is the Great Leader wearing an army uniform?" came a voice to my left.

It was true: Chairman Mao was dressed in an olive-green military uniform, the exact type favored by the Guards. No one had seen him dressed in uniform for many years. Turning away from Tiananmen Square and toward Gold Water Bridge, Mao didn't ascend the tower immediately. Instead, he took off the army cap he was wearing, lifted it high in the air, and waved to the crowd with it.

I'd been too caught up in the moment to notice what he was wearing, but now I tried to work out the reason Mao had chosen to wear an army uniform. What message did he want to convey, and to whom? Was it that he'd take a place on the front lines? With the support of the army, he was absolutely capable of waging and winning a war—if it came to war, that is.

His plan that day was simple but effective—and it would astonish the world. Instead of issuing instructions to the Party and government officials, he would give them directly to the masses, beginning with the country's youth. The students would revolt from the bottom up, setting off the Cultural Revolution that his rival, President Shaoqi, had sought in every way to prevent.

As soon as the rally began at 7:30 a.m., it was obvious that Liu Shaoqi's status had changed. As the second most powerful person in China, he had always stood beside Mao at every public appearance, but this time he was left behind.

He stood off to the side of the stage, glowering.

In his place stood two other figures, Zhou Enlai and Lin Biao. "I have two chief assistants," said Mao later, "Zhou Enlai, the civic one, and Lin Biao, the military. . .They are my left and right hands, and they also guarantee the success of the Cultural Revolution."

Lin Biao, Mao's closest comrade-in-arms, addressed the crowd first. As one of the major figures in the People's Liberation Army, he had led many outstanding military exploits, becoming an army commander at the age of twenty-three and working his way up through many successful campaigns to the rank of marshal. After the founding of the New China, he successively served as the CCP vice chairman, vice premier of the State Council, Defense Minister, and the first vice chairman of the CCP Military Commission. He was also the first to engender the personality cult of Mao in the army. He was so highly regarded that the words "we sincerely wish assistant commander-in-chief Lin Biao will always enjoy good health" was heard after each iteration of "we sincerely wish Chairman Mao a long life."

His brilliant military career notwithstanding, Lin Biao was a mystery. Some people described him as "an angel and devil in one." Who knew at that time that his life would end in just five years? Right then, he was dressed in a well-cut marshal's uniform, yellow in color. He spoke with a strong Hubei accent. Every sentence had a long-drawn ending. His voice was by no means pleasant, but it was very powerful.

"We're on your side," he said to the million students and Red Guards in the square. "You are courageous, pioneering, and you dare to revolt and engage yourselves in revolutionary work. This is the proletarian revolutionary spirit. Down with all capitalist road-takers among our authorities, all capitalist academic authorities, all capitalist royalists, and all sorts of bad people who are against the revolution!"

Cheers rose up from the Red Guards.

"We must do away with the exploiting class," Lin Biao continued, "their old ideology, old culture, old customs and habits, as well as everything in the superstructure they left behind to stand against a socialist economic base. We must sweep aside all evils and remove all obstacles in our road."

Toward the end of his speech, his voice took on a forbidding tone. "This is an important campaign," he maintained, "an all-round attack on the capitalist class and old ideology of the exploiting class. Under the leadership of Chairman Mao, we must launch the most destructive action against capitalist ideology, old customs, and habits. We must overthrow all capitalist right-wingers and authorities, completely discrediting them with no chance for a comeback."

In contrast to the many feverish speeches of that day, Zhou Enlai's words at the August 1966 rally were calm and well-reasoned. Later it would emerge that he privately opposed the Cultural Revolution, but he felt there was nothing he could do to change Mao's mind. When he spoke, he sounded like a wise but helpless old man.

"All revolutionaries," Zhou Enlai told the Red Guards, "should serve the people heart and soul. . .before working as their teachers. We are firmly against 'taking on what should be done by others,' against acting like a master issuing orders from above to the masses."

Zhou Enlai was premier of the State Council for twenty-six years, from the founding of the New China until his death in 1976. With his admirable political wisdom and charming personality, he drew universal praise both before and after his death. To the Chinese people, Zhou Enlai was unselfish and hardworking, wholly dedicated to the country and the people. A well-known writer once said of him, "To the billion Chinese, Zhou Enlai was the first perfect man."

His reputation extended beyond China. Former United Nations Secretary-General Dag Hammarskjold, after meeting Zhou Enlai, made what became a very popular remark: "Compared with Zhou Enlai, we are close to barbarians." Former U.S. president Richard Nixon declared: "Without Chairman Mao, no revolutionary fire would be set in China; without Zhou Enlai, everyone would have died in that fire." Before the founding of the New China, Stalin said to Mao: "You will be fine when founding your government because you have a premier ready: Zhou Enlai. Could there be a better candidate?" Former British Foreign Minister Robert Anthony Eden told a group of American journalists: "Zhou Enlai is unusual, and you will see it sooner or later." And finally there was Jacqueline Kennedy, President Kennedy's wife, who had a more direct assessment: "The only one I adore in this world is Zhou Enlai."

Mao also spoke highly of him. He had once worked under

Zhou, but after discovering Mao's unusual abilities, Zhou volunteered to work under Mao. After that, the men were absolutely loyal to each other. During the Cultural Revolution, Mao once said to Wang Hongwen, the leader of a group of rebels from Shanghai (later promoted to vice chairman of the CCP Central Committee), "The People won't allow anyone to act against Zhou Enlai." At one point, some Red Guards suggested to Mao that they "criticize and struggle against" Zhou Enlai, but Mao replied, "In that case, I will go with him." Later Mao would broaden his defense of Zhou: "If Premier Zhou is down, who can govern the state? No! Having him denounced? The People won't allow it!"

Zhou had voiced concern over the rally. He told Mao that "too many college and middle-school students have come to Beijing. Some of the Beijing students are worried about the ongoing educational reform. Its process might be slowed down. Also, lodging, boarding, and transportation are difficult for so many people. Getting back to class before September will be difficult."

Mao was not in the least perturbed. "Don't worry," he said. "It's still early and the masses have just begun to move. The Cultural Revolution needs contacts. Didn't we do it when we were young, and we came together? The firearms of the Northern Warlords could do nothing when students nationwide united." A rally like this, Mao asserted, should draw hundreds of thousands of Red Guards, and he was ready to greet them. Why? It was a lesson from the Soviet Union that must be learned. "Not many people in the Soviet Union had a chance to see Lenin," he exclaimed, "and this, among other things, spelled the end for Leninism."

By the time of the August 18th Rally, Zhou Enlai was already sixty-eight years old. As the premier, he had to keep the peace and order of the country in mind. But under pressure from Mao, how could he stay out of this political storm? Unity, he maintained, was the key. "Revolutionary students from Beijing and the rest of the country coming to Beijing should learn from each other, support each other, exchange notes, and strengthen unity."

The words were lost on many, if not most, of the crowd. Already some of the Red Guards had left, bent on "smashing" vestiges of China's pre-revolutionary past and punishing those standing in the way of Mao's vision. As for the others, they were not far behind.

My moment had finally come.

The Red Guards had finished their speeches and were now marching past the Tiananmen rostrum, drumming and gonging as they went. Some sang to the rhythm of bamboo clippers as they passed the tower. Everywhere I looked there was chaos and fervor.

Suddenly I saw him: Chairman Mao. He was walking in my direction. He came closer and closer until he reached the southwestern corner of the handrails. Then, he took off the army cap he was wearing, which he then waved to people down below and to us on the western viewing stand.

Standing just a dozen meters away, I nearly fainted from excitement. "Long Live Chairman Mao!" I belted out.

My eyes were glued to him. I was surprised to see that his army uniform looked too small on his heavy body. Would one of the buttons pop loose? Oddly, this irreverent concern didn't diminish my excitement.

Every one of us was now jumping and dancing. A girl next to me looked as if she was possessed by a supernatural force. From the beginning of the rally to this moment, she'd been continuously jumping and shouting, tears streaming down her face. Her fervor—and the crowd's—stoked my own.

I would pay a price for this wild excitement—the next morning, my back hurt terribly. "Did someone beat you?" my mother asked when she saw the bruises on my body. I was confused for a moment, until I realized what I had done the previous day: I must have punched and beaten the back of the person standing in front of me and whoever was behind me must have done the same to me.

Now came the most unforgettable moment of all: Song Binbin placed a Red Guard armband on Mao's arm. Song Binbin was a student at the girls' school at Beijing Normal University and the daughter of Song Renqiong, an army general who had helped found New China. As the leader of the Red Guards at her school, she certainly deserved this honor. The armband was hers, and it would now be given to Chairman Mao.

As Chairman Mao accepted the gift from Song Binbin, journalists around them snapped their camera shutters to record the moment. The resulting photographs would become a classic emblem of the Cultural Revolution.

The news that Mao was now sporting a Red Guard

armband exploded through the crowds, blasting down the rostrum and into the square. Apart from the Red Guard organizations at Tsinghua Middle School, other student groups appeared in Beijing to counter the pressure and hostility of President Shaoqi's people. Many of these students had been blacklisted, and their fate was hanging in the balance.

Not anymore. By wearing the armband, Chairman Mao had sent a clear message: He was on the students' side. He supported the Red Guards. He supported us.

The cheers quickly turned into slogans: "We are Chairman Mao's Red Guards and he is our Red Commander!" Even the voice from the loudspeakers trembled with excitement: "Our respected and beloved Chairman Mao, we have etched your teachings in our minds. We will carry arms from the previous generation to safeguard our socialist system. We are not afraid of pioneering and revolting. We are courageous enough to take upon any revolutionary job, and with you as our leader, we have nothing to be afraid of!"

After accepting the Red Guard armband, Mao exchanged a few words with Song Binbin:

"Does your first name mean one who is academic, gentle, and polite?"

"Yes."

"But you know that to be a fighter, you must also be courageous, right?"

"I will be," Song Binbin replied.

Mao was right about the necessity of courage, but such courage would come at a horrific cost. Once it was stimulated, the new spirit of rebellion would totally control our minds. Psychologists call this phenomenon "Lucifer," alluding to the chief spirit of evil and a rebel against God. Within certain circumstances, a young person with a previously "normal" psychology can be transformed into a torturer in a matter of days.

The events to come would reveal a stunning but incontrovertible truth: many thousands of "Lucifers" were born that night.

Looking out onto the ecstatic crowd that day in Tiananmen Square must have sent a chill down Liu Shaoqi's spine.

Peng Xiaomeng, one of the Red Guards, was just seventeen years old when she met Liu Shaoqi at the August rally. She insisted on giving him her red armband to show her respect. She had no idea what an awkward situation this put him in as president of the republic. In the end, Liu Shaoqi swallowed his bitterness and accepted the armband, only to tear it off as soon as she left.

Tension was palpable inside the Communist Party lounge that night. Huge sofas occupied the center of the room, flanked on either side by long conference tables. Mao often retreated to this space to rest and reflect, and it was here that he went after the rally in Tiananmen Square.

When Liu entered the room and passed Mao, neither of them acknowledged the other. For his part, Mao was quite at ease, smoking and reading his newspaper. Liu Shaoqi took a seat by himself across the room.

"Usually," Zhou Enlai's doctor later recalled, "Liu Shaoqi would have many high-level officials around him to speak with, at least coming up to greet him. Now, Liu Shaoqi was obviously cold-shouldered. Nobody came up to start a conversation."

But there were exceptions. One of them was Wu Xiuquan, the assistant general chief of staff of the PLA, who was quickly removed from his post after this event and jailed for eight years. After the Cultural Revolution, he became the chief judge in the trial against Madame Mao, Mao's wife. He was one of the few who went up to Liu Shaoqi after the rally.

"I inquired about his health," Wu Xiuquan recalled, "before we moved on to talk about the ongoing Cultural Revolution. He didn't understand what was happening. This was what I learned from what he said. He had read Nie Yuanzi's big-character poster more than once, he said, but failed to recognize why people thought it was more significant than the *Manifesto of the Paris Commune*. In this, I felt the same. But I couldn't speak my mind. I just said that I hadn't had time to read it carefully, which I planned to do later."

But already it was too late for such measures. The chess game between Chairman Mo and Liu Shaoqi was nearly at its end.

Until now, Liu Shaoqi had been confident, sure that victory would be his, but Mao's stunt—drawing a million young students and Red Guards to his side in Tiananmen Square—changed everything. Together with the Red Guards, millions of young students—and the general public—turned into pieces on his chessboard.

Years later I learned that the million people at Tiananmen Square were just the tip of the iceberg. One billion Chinese people had attended or knew someone who'd attended similar rallies all across the country. Every factory, village, school, army camp, and governmental and business department was instructed to listen to the Tiananmen Square rally from loudspeakers. The rally was therefore not attended by a million people, but by hundreds of millions. In every sense, that rally was the largest in human history.

In two years, Liu Shaoqi would be among the leaders denounced by the Red Guards. In three years, he would die while in their custody. All that was still a ways off, but from that night on, Liu Shaoqi knew that he had lost the game. China belonged to Mao.

Yet the wild success of the August 1966 rally would prove a double-edged sword for the Chairman. To the millions of young people mobilized to revolt, it was an extraordinary day in Chinese history. From that day the fire of revolution blazed across the country for almost ten years. But Mao never expected that with that fire, the situation would spiral out of control. He didn't know that the fire he'd ignited would eventually consume everything, even him. Nor did the rest of the country know that the most precious things— including independent thinking and our rich cultural history—would be the first to be destroyed.

'REBELLION IS ALWAYS RIGHT'

THE AUGUST 18TH RALLY CHANGED THE COURSE OF CHINESE history. The most incredible short-term development came from the Ministry of Public Security, which asked its local bureaus to supply the Red Guards with the names of all those belonging to the "black five categories": landlords, rich peasants, anti-revolutionaries, bad people of other kinds, and right-wingers. This, the ministry said, was so that students could more easily identify, humiliate, and punish those who ran afoul of the party.

With this authorization, the police took the country's millions of Red Guards under their wing. From now on the Red Guards' actions, however heinous, were not only sanctioned but encouraged. This authorization paved the way to the climax of the Red Guard movement, which took place in August of that year. People would in time describe that month as the "Red Terror."

Between August and late-September 1966, two thousand

people were killed in Beijing alone. "They deserve death after cutting themselves off from the Party and the People!" the killers declared. Unmoored from reason and unburdened by fears of punishment, the Red Guards now justified even the most violent acts as righteous revolutionary behavior. Brutality was necessary to "keep the proletarian authorities red forever."

I would never torture my teachers—or anyone else—but I would witness some of the worst brutalities of those days. When every voice in China, even those of the authorities, shouted "Revolt is right!" I joined the cries. Later, when my classmates tortured our teachers with leather belts, clubs, and wooden sticks, my eyes went cold. I looked away when teachers were paraded on the streets with trash cans on their heads. I tried not to see how they were beaten—sometimes even to death.

August and September of that year were the worst for teachers at my school. Zhang Chengjiu was the first to collapse. It happened on the exercise grounds. All the "bad people" had been instructed to run on the track. It was a punishingly hot day, and Mr. Chengjiu was quite overweight and out of shape. He'd been forced to run for days. On this day, after a dozen laps, he was unable to continue. He dropped to the ground, and he couldn't get up again. Most of the eyes around were cold and callous; some were even gleeful. There were a few with guilty looks, but by now it was too late to stop what was happening.

Yao Shuxi was the next target. In her forties, she had never been married. She lived on the fifth floor of the dorm building for faculty members. At one struggle session, her head had been wedged between the legs of a chair as large groups of students took turns beating her. During the time of her vilification and punishment, a worker at the school by the name of Liu Guilan was beaten to death because of her family background. Together with several others, Yao Shuxi was ordered to carry the corpse into a truck.

Lin Yian, a faculty member at my school, later published an essay entitled "One Night in the Cultural Revolution" in the influential magazine, *Southern Weekly*. An astonishingly detailed account, it recorded the events after Liu Guilan was killed, how the author and some others carried her body onto a truck, and what followed after the truck arrived at the crematorium.

> It was a hot and suffocating summer afternoon in August (I can't remember the date exactly), when the first and second groups of faculty members sentenced to reform through labor were working on the toilet on the eastern side of the campus. Some were weeding, others, sweeping the grounds. Everyone was sweating all over—I was one of them—when two Red Guards in army uniforms came to us, each with a wide army belt doubled up in hand. I stole a glance at them; they were aged 15 or 16. Their childlike faces had a malicious look on them. I had seen one of them before. He was an Arabic major in the third grade of middle school. "We need two people to carry corpses," one of them barked, pointing his finger at Cheng Bi, our Party committee secretary, and Mo Ping, the school principal. "You two, come tonight."

All of us were taken aback. Who had died? At our confused expressions, the two Red Guards said contemptuously, "It was Liu Guilan from a land-owner's family. We need to dispose of her body this evening." Liu Guilan! We looked at each other, confused. Wasn't that the janitor for the kinder-garten? I knew her. She had been transferred from the foreign teachers' offices. As a Spanish teacher, I was often in and out of our foreign workers' office, and frequently bumped into Liu Guilan. To me, she was a gentle, hard-working, fair-skinned, ordinary-looking young woman, always dressed neatly and nice to everyone. For some reason, nobody knew why she was transferred to the kindergarten. As a willful person, she never went out of her way to please anyone. If she saw something was wrong, she would speak up before anybody else did. Probably because of her character she had some enemies at school. At that time, she was only in her mid-20s. How could she have been killed as a woman from a landowner's family? At our perplexed looks, the two Red Guards shouted, "You two, Lei Li and Cheng Bi, report to the tool storage room this evening."

Lei Li was tall and big, while Cheng Bi, a small and thin old lady [actually, she was just in her 40s]. She had lost half of her hair, and many ink stains had been purposely splashed on her clothing. A couple of days earlier, one of her legs had been injured by the Red Guards. Have her carry corpses? They must have been joking! So I went up to the two young-sters saying, "Leave Cheng Bi alone, let me do the job." Giving me an odd look, the two agreed.

Back at the dorm I was told the details. Liu Guilan had been whipped to death with leather belts, publicly, in the open ground before the auditorium. The Red Guards did the whipping again and again in a leisurely manner as if they had all the time in the world. Liu Guilan died before she could breast-feed her baby, and her breasts were swollen to the point of bursting. Instead of asking for mercy, she angrily shouted at the torturers. The infuriated Red Guards aimed at her breasts, landing each whiplash with all their might. She rolled over and over on the ground in pain, then convulsed before breathing her last. According to hearsay, the Red Guards had known nothing about her family background until someone from the school clinic, one of her enemies, slipped them the information.

I was then in my 30s, the youngest among the inmates. The other people were either in their 40s or 50s, some even nearly 60. I wanted to risk everything to taste this "great and unprecedented Cultural Revolution." After supper, I went to the place I was told, the storage room west of the logistics department office. Lei Li was already there, having brought along a used bed cover. It was for the corpse, he said. He had been very cooperative ever since the Cultural Revolution began. He did his utmost when laboring. Even when his teenage daughter—prompted by some evil-minded fellow students—had spread salt on the wound inflicted by Red Guards on his head, he said nothing.

It was already dark when the two Red Guards rushed in. With the key they'd brought, they opened the door. "Go in and take it out," they instructed. Inside the room, by a very dim light, we saw Liu Guilan's blood-stained body lying sideways on the ground, a pair of plastic sandals, no socks, on her feet. It gave off a stinking odor. Lei Li knew what he was doing, for he spread out the bed cover, with which he wrapped up the body from head to foot. He held one end and I, the other. We carried the body, as instructed, to a jeep parked in the passageway. Upon arriving at the crematorium, we unloaded the jeep at the brandishing of belts. We were met with the strong stench of disinfectant fluid. The people who worked there showed us into a larger room, motioning us to leave the body on the floor. We did, and thought the job was over. But we were wrong, for a belt landed heavily on my back before the Red Guards barked, "Do a circuit around the walls!" As we were doing so, with all the caution we could exercise, more threats came: "You dare to disobey orders? This is what you will end up like!"

After the rounds, we thought the nightmare was over. Once again, we were wrong. The sound of screaming truck wheels came from outside. Before the trucks came to a complete halt, about twenty teenage Red Guards jumped out. By the time they'd exchanged a couple of words with those two who'd come along with us, we knew our nightmare was far from over. Several of them came up to us, waist belts in hand. "You two," they pointed at us, "come up and join them." Following their fingers we saw people on the trucks starting to unload sacks. We understood. There were corpses inside. My brain did a silent count: at least ten sacks for a truck, and there were five trucks, forty or fifty altogether, which meant fifty people had been killed. Before I recovered from the shock, one of the Red Guards shouted, "Hurry up or you'll be one of them!" Lei Li and I, together with the people unloading the trucks—"bad people," of course—moved hurriedly. Each sack was heavy. I kept track of the number of the sacks Lei Li and I moved. It was nine, Liu Guilan included.

After the job was done, Lei Li and I stood still at the doorway waiting for further instructions. At our meek subjection, the two Red Guards who had come with us were satisfied. With a lash of the whip on each of us, one of them said, "Good job. Now take your asses back to where you came from!" By the same jeep, we returned. Finally, eventually, at last, the nightmare was over. Was that all, the forty or fifty that evening? I doubted it. How many had been killed that night? How had these teenagers become fiends overnight?

People say crematoriums are portals to either Hell or Heaven. What I saw had nothing to do with Heaven, only Hell!

Not long after this, Yao Shuxi killed herself by hanging herself in the public toilet on the third floor of our school. "I was unable to endure any longer," she wrote in her suicide note. But the humiliation still didn't stop. By committing suicide she had "alienated herself from the Party and the people." This was a phrase often heard on students' lips at the time. Did the Red Guards need to "approve" of suicides? I wondered. And by killing themselves would they now be doubly condemned?

That August, violence spread like a plague, as did suicide. On August 17, more than ten teachers from the famous Middle School Number 101 were dragged out of their classrooms to be tortured. They were made to crawl on a path paved with coal cinder until their hands and feet bled profusely. They were lashed with studded army belts. A female Red Guard in heavy boots stepped on one teacher's hands. Also at that school, art lecturer Chen Baokun was savagely beaten, then thrown into a pond and drowned.

Two days later, I heard, Red Guards dragged about twenty "bad people" from different schools and ordered them to kneel in line inside the concert hall at Zhongshan Park. There they were slapped, punched, kicked and whipped with army belts. Among the "bad people" was the chief of the Education Bureau of the Beijing Municipal Government. He lost three ribs, but he survived. Wen Han, vice principal of Middle School Number Eight, was dragged there to the park with a rope tied around his neck. The other end of the rope was held by a Red Guard on a bicycle. Covered head to foot in blood, he finally lost consciousness as his body was dragged up to the stage.

Xu Pikai, a middle school principal, was tied to a tree and Red Guards practiced thrusting wooden rods at his body. He lost several ribs. Jiang Nanxiang, Minister of Education and President of Tsinghua University, was not spared. After his home was ransacked, he was made to kneel, his head pinned to the ground under someone's foot, while being whipped with army belts. Not happy with the pattern of the wounds left on his back—they weren't symmetrical enough—they descended with their whips a second time.

The death toll rose rapidly. A thirty-six year-old Chinese language teacher from Middle School Number 52 was killed. A biology lecturer from the middle school under Beijing Normal University was knocked to the ground in her office by Red Guards before being dragged out by her legs, her head bumping against the concrete steps along the way. She died two hours later after being savagely beaten outside the office building. Still not satisfied, the torturers made the rest of teachers form a ring to strike the body, one by one.

Outside of Beijing, other areas also saw savage torture. Not a single school, according to later investigations, escaped violence that summer.

Much to my surprise, girls proved no less—if not more—violence-prone than the boys. Actually, the first teacher killed that August had taught in the girls' school under Beijing Normal University. Song Binbin was the head of the Red Guards there. She was later received by Chairman Mao on Tiananmen Tower, during which time she put a Red Guard band on his arm. After enquiring after her name, which meant "gentle and scholarly," Chairman Mao suggested she change it. "Why not make it a military name?" he proposed. Not only did the girl get a new name, but also her school was renamed to "Yao Wu Middle School," meaning "Fearlessly Military." Before long, on the afternoon of August 5, during the drive of "fighting against bad people," three vice principals and two deans of students lost their lives at that school. Both the torturers and spectators had Red Guard bands on their arms. They poured ink over the five victims, dunce-capped them, hung plaques on their necks, and after making them kneel, started savagely beating them with cudgels and sticks. They even poured boiling water onto their bodies. The first one down after three hours of torture was Principal Bian Zhongyun. The cart with her body was left unattended on campus for two hours. By the time it arrived at the hospital, she was pronounced long-dead. She had worked at the school for seventeen years.

The perpetrators had all been girls. According to statistics, violence conducted by girls occurred frequently nationwide. Once they started, they often appeared more bloodthirsty than the boys.

✩✩✩

Death was all around me that summer, but one day I faced it head-on.

On that day, a girl ran out of the bathroom, crying hysterically at the top of her voice, "Help, help!" Some of the more thuggish male students rushed downstairs to see what was going on. A man, the girl told them breathlessly, was hiding inside the women's restroom. Seconds later, the culprit was found. A man was dragged out. It was a peasant from a nearby village. Before he could explain that he'd come to collect waste for fertilizer, he'd already been knocked down.

A large group of us went to see what was happening. It was a savage beating, totally ruthless and uninhibited. I felt a lurch at each strike. For a brief moment Lu Xun's short story *Medication* came to mind. The people in the story stick out their chins while watching an execution; they look like ducks held up by their necks. I felt like one of those people in the story—so callous, so cold and so numb. I didn't like the feeling, so I turned and left.

The peasant was dead before too long. The smell of blood carried through the school. Of all the cases of killing I'd heard about, none was like this; it happened right before my eyes. A life had been taken. My heart was hammering and it would not stop.

At that time, there were three Red Guard organizations on our campus, and most of the violence was conducted by only one of them, the "Red Guards of Mao Zedongism." The other two were relatively reserved, made up of students from either workers' or intellectuals' families. Even the Red Guards of Mao Zedongism were not all the same. A split occurred later in September of that year. Some from high-ranking officials' families became rational. They even formed a team to break up fights.

"Isn't the Central Party Committee against violence?" I asked once during this time. A group of us were discussing the latest events at our school. "Why do we beat people?"

A gentle-looking bespectacled girl student offered a quick reply: "You were there for the Ten Thousand People's Debate. Didn't Madame Mao support Peng Xiaomeng when he beat someone right then and there, on the stage? Madame Mao even embraced Peng Xiaomeng afterwards. Didn't Madame Mao say, 'rebellion is always right' and 'revolutionaries come with me, anti-revolutionaries get out'?"

There was no arguing with her, but I felt that somehow I should take a stand. After the peasant was killed, two schoolmates and I posted a big-character poster, calling on students "not to fight with force, not to beat people and not to ransack homes."

Not long after that, a Chinese language teacher in her thirties was beaten for having come from a family of land-owners. She was forced to confess how much money her family had taken away from poor peasants. More than once she dropped to her knees begging for mercy, to no avail. A piece of flesh was cut from her ear with a nail affixed to a cudgel. She started bleeding profusely. Towards dusk she looked like she was about to collapse. At this, the Red Guards kicked her out.

With her hand cupped over the wound, she approached
a student at the senior high school for help. He didn't
hesitate, and neither did I. He managed to get a large tricycle, which we used to take the teacher to hospital. The
student held the teacher on the cart and we set off. It was
my first time riding a tricycle and I was so clumsy that the
moment we were out of the gate I bumped into a wall.
Luckily, before long I got the hang of it. The teacher
murmured along the way, saying how she had dropped to
her knees for mercy but that her torturers hadn't stopped.
It was getting dark by the time we finally got her to a nearby
hospital.

I helped saved that teacher's life, but there were many
others I couldn't save and would never forget.

To the Red Guards, the several-hundred-year-old Forbidden City was the ultimate symbol of the "Four Olds." Its northern entrance, the Gate of Divine Prowess, was renamed "Palace of Blood and Tears," but Premier Zhou Enlai's intervention prevented the Forbidden City's destruction.

Books, deemed a means of propagating the "Four Olds," were seized, burned, and destroyed during the Cultural Revolution.

SMASH THE FOUR OLDS

"SMASH THE FOUR OLDS." WHENEVER I THINK OF THESE WORDS, the phrase that most readily comes to mind is "cultural suicide." More than any other phrase or slogan, these words encapsulate one of the most senseless campaigns waged during the Cultural Revolution: the ruthless and systemic destruction of the country's history and culture.

In 1966, Chairman Mao exhorted young Red Guards to "Smash the Four Olds": old customs, old culture, old habits, and old ideas. I'd witness countless instances of such "smashing," but none would have quite the force as the story of Mother's high-heeled shoes.

It was a day toward the end of August. The Red Guards' campaign to "Smash the Four Olds" had only recently begun. Both Father and Mother were at work, and I was at home tinkering with my crystal radio set.

I was surprised when Father bought me the radio set. At

the time I didn't understand his intention. More and more, he had been urging me to put more effort into my schoolwork. I'd long since wanted to build a radio, only to be refused. Later I'd realize that in order to keep me safe, Father was determined to keep me at home more often. The radio was a part of that plan, and it worked.

Immersed in my tinkering, I suddenly heard my sister call out to me from downstairs. "Brother, come down quickly!" she shouted. I leapt to the window and saw her running toward the compound gate, her pigtails bouncing from side to side. Mother was limping along behind here.

Something was terribly wrong. I rushed downstairs, only to see my mother approaching with her shoes in her hands. Her feet were bare and she was in obvious pain.

I was horrified. "What happened?"

She waved the shoes at me and said one breathless word: "Afraid."

I took the shoes from her and helped her up the stairs.

Her shoes had been battered. A pair of delicate plimsolls, the shoes were a pale green color with two-inch heels. They had been a wedding anniversary gift from Father. Mother treasured them. She had come to Beijing with them on her feet.

Only when we were back home and the door was closed behind us did Mother tell us what had happened: While she was waiting for a bus, a couple of Red Guards came up to her and began angrily accusing her of leading a "bourgeois lifestyle." Their proof was her high-heeled shoes.

The Guards made Mother take them off and then they smashed the heels with their hammers. Her treasure was no more. She walked all the way back home barefoot.

"Why?" Mother kept murmuring as she scrubbed the dirt from her bare feet. Tears streamed down her cheeks. "Why, why, why?"

✵✵✵

According to the *People's Daily* at the time, the campaign to "Smash the Four Olds" served "to eliminate the poisons of the old ideology, culture, customs, and habits left by the exploiting classes that have polluted the working classes for several thousand years." In order to bring education, art, and literature in line with Communist ideology, anything that was suspected of being feudal or bourgeois was to be destroyed.

"The Chinese New Year is an old custom," I once said to Father. "Should we still observe it?"

After thinking for a moment, he replied tactfully, "Let's wait and see when the festival comes."

During the most chaotic years of the Cultural Revolution, there was no celebration for the New Year at all. Red banners, which for 1,000 years had borne couplets about springtime and prosperity, now had to feature revolutionary slogans lauding Chairman Mao. Temple fairs vanished, lion and dragon dances were scorned, gifts forbidden.

But what, I wondered, was so wrong with the New Year? I wasn't the only one who found the "Smash the Four Olds" concept confusing. No one ever seemed to come up with a clear-cut rationale for the campaign.

That didn't stop the Red Guards, though. Over the next

few years, they would ravage untold numbers of historical sites, precious art works, and age-old traditions in the name of eradicating China of the "Four Olds."

The Red Guards from Beijing's Middle School Number Two were the first to "smash." On August 19, 1966, more than three thousand of them took to the streets, putting up big-character posters to "declare war on the old world." They would "destroy all the places that served the capitalist class," they asserted, "including but not limited to barbers, tailors, photo studios, and privately-owned bookstores."

Young people should get rid of their Hong Kong-style clothing, ditch their fashionable hairstyles, and burn "obscene" books and photos. Some further tips were provided: jeans could be cut into shorts, and the cut-off parts could be used as patches when they needed mending; pointy-tip leather shoes could be used as sandals after their tips were cut off; high-heeled shoes could be fashioned into flats; and, if you didn't want to burn them, objectionable books, magazines, posters, and photographs could be dropped off at the dump.

"We will take care of all breaches," the Red Guards announced, adding that they would "mend even the smallest crevices on the wall of ideology and eliminate all revisionist hotbeds—and in this, we will be very ruthless!"

This statement mobilized thousands of other Red Guards in Beijing. The next day, the original declaration appeared at our school in the form of a big-character poster on the wall outside the students' canteen. As I read it, my heart quickened. It was my duty to save the nation, I thought. I wanted to start right away. Much to my dismay, nobody was willing to take me along on "Smash the Four Olds" rounds. Some of the older boys even laughed and mocked me in front of the girls.

"You want to tag along? Why don't you learn proper standard Chinese first!"

I was furious—and hurt. Just a few days later, when Mother limped home barefoot after her high heels were wrecked in the streets, I lost my interest in tagging along to "Smash the Four Olds," but I couldn't quite shrug off the feeling of rejection. It would stay with me a long time—that and the conviction that I had to live up to my ideal of a young revolutionary.

✷✷✷

In the beginning, the Red Guards did no more than "put things right" whenever they saw long hair, high-heeled shoes, or jeans, but this proved a mere warm-up for the vicious acts to come.

After Mother was humiliated in the street, I gave up my membership to the Red Guards of Maoism, one of the more radical organizations that had sprung up in the wake of the August 18th rally in Tiananmen Square. I was still devoted to the revolution, but I was eager to find a different outlet. An opportunity soon emerged: There was a spot open at the school newspaper, *Jinggangshan*.

I applied and was accepted. There were five of us working on the paper; the other four were seniors in high school. I was the only one from middle school—a kid compared to the others, but my writing was good. To me, working on a stencil plate or mimeographing was a piece of cake. But working on the school paper had other advantages. As a correspondent, I would have the opportunity to mix with upperclassmen. I could help copy big-character posters, check out what was happening in the city, and learn about things I'd never heard of before.

By now the Red Guards had feverishly embraced "Smash the Four Olds." Bent on destruction, they were busy destroying anything related to history and art that they could find. The Guards could also hold anyone at will for questioning, torture, even death. Not only did they act with impunity, their acts were openly encouraged. Editorials published in *Red Banner* magazine and the *People's Daily*—two mouthpieces of the Communist Party of China—lauded the Red Guards' most maniacal actions. "We are behind the actions of the Red Guards, quite supportive of their revolutionary spirit," they announced. "With Mao Thought as their weapon, these Red Guards are fighting the old culture, habits, and customs. What they are doing is highly inspiring."

Even the law sided with the Red Guards. A decree issued from the Ministry of Public Security to law enforcement bodies across the country proclaimed: "There is no excuse to suppress the action of revolutionary students, and no police presence should ever be seen on campus; no one is to be arrested without proof of murder, arson, poisoning, sabotaging public facilities, or stealing classified information of the state."

The campaign quickly took on a new character in Beijing. Homes were ransacked and their occupants tortured. Many students in our school came from revolutionary families; it would be difficult to attack them without some sort of proof. It wasn't long before some students found a means of routing out enemies. Student records were locked inside a storage room, but one day the door to the storage room was kicked open. Fresh targets emerged.

"Did you hear what happened?" a classmate named Min asked me one day. We worked on the school paper together, but we'd only exchanged a few words until then. I shook my head. "The father of one of the students here was a business owner before New China was founded. Their house is in the center of town and. . ."

I felt my heart drop. "Yes?"

"It's been ransacked."

After a silence, Min continued. "And now," she said, "Red Guards from several middle schools are planning to attack the Quanjude Roast Duck Restaurant." She told me she would be covering the event for the school paper. "Do you want to come along?"

I felt a now-familiar mixture of excitement and dread. "Yes," I said quickly. "Absolutely."

"Good, but remember to keep your mouth shut but your eyes open."

We mounted our bicycles, racing through the city streets, but when we reached Quanjude nobody was around. Qianmen was a famous shopping street in Beijing, but the ongoing Cultural Revolution had drained much of the business away.

"We must be early," Min said.

On a whim, I suggested taking a look at the home of the

girl who'd been targeted. What was the situation there? It was just a short distance away, I said, and we'd be back in no time.

We looked around for several minutes, but we couldn't find the right place. Unexpectedly, however, we came across a group of Red Guards ransacking another family's property.

The victims were a couple in the leather and fur business. Their goods flew onto the street like birds from inside the yard. Before long, both of them—they were in their fifties—were dragged outside and made to drop on their knees in the yard. The woman, her face ashen, seemed on the edge of a nervous collapse. Great beads of sweat dripped from the man's face.

"Now face east!" shouted a bespectacled Red Guard. East was the correct direction for pleading guilty, because the red sun, Chairman Mao, rose there.

The couple did as they were told, shaking all the while.

Next a female student in an army cap and two long plaits stepped forward. She slipped a studded leather belt loose from her wait, raised it in the air, and began lashing the couple with it. A sickening feeling came over me as I realized she wore that belt so that she could beat people with it. She did this self-righteously, as if she were enjoying it.

"Why did you exploit people?" she berated the couple between lashes.

Mother's ravaged high-heels came to mind. Before I could say anything, someone gripped my arm. It was Min. Her face looked stricken and she seemed to have forgotten herself. When she realized what she'd done, she awkwardly loosened her grip.

She was a top student in her class, and a lovely girl, but she had a reputation for being prickly. She turned to me. At that moment her eyes held no trace of coldness. When her eyelashes flickered, they were like lightning in a night sky. I saw something there in her gaze. It suggested nothing, or perhaps anything.

We were almost out of the crowd when we heard a loud thump from behind us. Looking back, I saw that the man had fallen on the ground, head first. A Red Guard stood behind him, his black boot still raised in the air. His head must have hit something sharp on the ground because blood was oozing from his ear.

Nobody went to help him. Instead, a male Red Guard continued kicking at him and shouting, "Quit playing the fool with us. Get up now!"

All at once Min cried out, "Stop!"

I was confused. Everyone was confused. She was taking an enormous risk in calling them out.

"Who is the leader here?" Min called out.

A boy, slightly older than the others, stepped forward. "Who are you?" he demanded, "and what do you want?"

"Make no mistake," Min said, "I'm all for your revolutionary actions." Then she quickly produced a letter of introduction from her pocket. As one of the first schools that had produced Red Guards in Beijing, our school—the Beijing Foreign Languages School—was fairly famous, and the boy must have heard of it. With that—and the Red Guard's armband on her arm—she established her qualifications to speak out.

"The Red Guards from Middle School Number Two,"

she began, "have demonstrated a revolutionary spirit of revolt. In a moment, they will come to remove the signboard of the Quanjude Roast Duck Restaurant, and you," my companion emphasized, "should go and join them."

The Red Guards from Middle School Number Two enjoyed a certain degree of notoriety, possibly owing to their famous big-character poster *The War Declared Upon the Old World*.

What Min said immediately aroused their interest.

"We all want to go!" one of them shouted.

"I have a suggestion," Min went on. "We should preserve the targets we are aiming for, don't you think?" At his confused look she pointed her finger at the man on the ground. He was bleeding profusely now. "This man is one of our targets," she said. "He may die unless we do something about his wound, meaning that we will lose our resource."

Targets for public denouncement were a resource? This idea was unheard of, but it sounded logical. With the promise of joint action with the famous Red Guards from Middle School Number Two, the boy gave his ready approval. Looking back, he barked, "Liu, send your father to hospital immediately or I will hold you responsible!"

At this, a very skinny young boy appeared from the crowd. As the boy helped his father to his feet, I realized that all that time he'd been in the crowd, watching everything.

Min and I returned to Qianmen Street, setting out for Quanjude Roast Duck Restaurant.

"You just wanted him to get to the hospital as soon as

possible, right?" I asked as soon as we were alone.

Shooting me a sly look, Min asked in return, "And what would you have said if I did?"

"My father once said that even revolutionaries should show some humanity, and what you did was just that."

At this, she broke into a smile and dimples deepened on her cheeks. This was the first time I had seen her smile, and when she did, she looked adorable. Why hadn't I noticed it before?

"Let's go," she said just then, tossing her head in the direction of the restaurant.

Quanjude was a hundred-year-old establishment famous for its unique roast duck. Today, you still can't say you've been to Beijing unless you've had roast duck at Quanjude. During the Cultural Revolution, Quanjude was deemed "feudalistic"—capitalist and revisionary—and thus a target for overzealous revolutionaries.

That day a throng of Red Guards stood at the doorways of many shops on Qianmen, gearing up to "Smash the Four Olds." Before long, a crowd of Guards approached from the direction of Tiananmen Square, large wooden boards in hand. As they marched, they shouted revolutionary slogans.

When they got to Quanjude, they stopped. On that day, united with the Red Guards from other schools, students from Middle School Number Two pried off the restaurant's distinctive signage.

They were met with resistance. The manager stood his ground, refusing to let them do away with the sign—and thus began an angry argument. What he said wasn't without reason: this was not a private business, but rather under the joint ownership of the government and private owners. In other words, Quanjude was a socialist enterprise.

Confronted by this logic, the Red Guards hesitated. They all looked over to a lean boy of medium height in an old army uniform, obviously their leader. Eventually the boy stepped up and said in a composed manner, "It is correct that you are a socialist business, but the name 'Quanjude' originates from the old society. Why do you keep it? Don't you have any class consciousness? Why don't you follow Chairman Mao's instructions? Why are you resisting the revolution?"

His voice was low and steady, but every word the boy said was forceful.

The manager was obviously tongue-tied and more than a little panic-stricken.

"Take it down," he told his workers, "and put it in the storeroom."

But the Red Guard was still not satisfied. "Do you want to keep it so that you can put it back up?" He shook his head and waved his cadre forward. "You go and take it down!"

The sign had been there for more than seventy years, with the restaurant's name written in gold on black, very cultural and historic. Within a couple of minutes, it had been smashed to pieces with hammers. As if not having had enough, some of the Guards rushed up to stamp on it with their boots.

By this point, all the restaurant workers had come out to the street to watch. Some looked aghast, others applauded.

This group of Red Guards came from different schools—even so, they cooperated with one another and had clearly come prepared, for they'd brought along a new sign which read "Beijing Roast Duck Restaurant." With the help of some workers, the board was swiftly fixed in place.

Is this what's meant by "Smash the Four Olds?" I asked myself. The new sign was far less impressive than the old one, which was now gone, destroyed. *What a pity*, I thought. I assumed the mission was now over, but smashing the sign was just the prelude to the show. To the Red Guards, the restaurant staff was riddled with old ideologies. They'd have to be taught a new way, a different way. The Guards stormed into the restaurant, gathering all the workers for a meeting to uplift their revolutionary awareness.

Min and I stayed and watched. By then, all the customers had gone, leaving the floor entirely to the Red Guards. The workers had clearly never had such an experience before. The cooks in their tall white hats came forward. They were visibly excited.

Once again it was the skinny Red Guard who started things off. "The old name of the business," he began, "is a lie. It advocates false virtues of wealth, which is just money that capitalists took away from working people. This change of name is a part of class struggle, a way to eliminate the vestiges of capitalism."

For a moment the staff was quiet, but all at once they broke out in applause. Delighted expressions appeared on every face, and with that, Quanjude was no more.

Similar scenes played out endlessly throughout the city. An editorial from the *People's Daily* celebrated the Red

Guards' newest initiative this way: "Beijing has been liberated from the reactionary government for seventeen years, but under the control of the former Beijing Municipal government, with its revisionist policies, the names of many restaurants, shops, and service trades still show feudalist and capitalist decadency. These names are poisoning the masses. How can we tolerate this? Where the broom does not reach, names are poisoning the masses. How can we tolerate this? Where the broom does not reach, the dust will not vanish in and of itself. Within just a couple of days, the Red Guards, with an iron broom, have cleaned up the country, doing away with old habits and customs left by the exploiting classes."

To the Red Guards, Beijing, as the capital city of China, would need to be completely rid of "stinking names left over from feudalism, capitalism, and revisionism." Chang'an Avenue, the major thoroughfare that crossed Tiananmen Square, became "The East is Red Street"; the old Legation Street to the east of Tiananmen became "Anti-Imperialism Road"; and due to the many foreign embassies there, Yangwei Road in front of the Soviet Union Embassy became "Anti-Revisionist Road" and Guanghua Road next to the Vietnamese Embassy became "Assisting Vietnam Road."

With so many new names popping up overnight, I felt as if I was suddenly living in a different city altogether. Even the name of the area where we lived, Weigongcun, was erased in favor of a new name. According to my father, the name was a translation from the Uygur language. This made sense. Many Uygur people made their home there. One day, I saw workers changing the road's name to "The Road to Serve the Public."

The street in front of Father's working unit, Baiwanzhuang Road, was also changed. The first two characters in the name meant "million." To the Red Guards, it sounded quite capitalist. So the name became "The Street of the Universe in Revolution." The street my school was on, Sanlihe Road, became "The Road of Revolutionary Friendship."

With so many alien names around them, the older residents of Beijing were confused and disoriented. But the renaming of the city went on. Shops, hospitals, and schools were next. The famous Wangfujing Shopping Center became "Beijing Department Store"; the well-known Union Hospital, originally founded and financed by U.S. and London church and missionary societies, became "Anti-Imperialism Hospital"; the old tailor from Shanghai changed his business' name to "Anti-Imperialism." Many leaders of the Party and State had their suits custom-tailored there. Zhou Enlai was said to have had seven suits made for him by the tailor. The old name was banned from use, and business went on as usual—more or less.

Some Red Guards even changed the names of their schools. The famous Middle School under Tsinghua University became "Red Guards School." One day, the faculty members and students of Suzhou Lane Primary posted a big-character poster in which they requested an urgent change: "The old name of the school is not revolutionary at all. Long March Primary School is more appropriate. It is what we want."

My own school was not left behind. One day at lunchtime, I heard some leaders of the Red Guards of

Maoism talking about the name of our school. "Foreign languages," one of them said, "are weapons with which to fight, also a means to spread Mao ideas across the world." Another one chipped in: "Of all the schools in Beijing, ours has more foreign languages taught than any other. To show the support of the nations in their struggles against U.S. imperialism and Soviet revisionism, why not give our school a more revolutionary name?" They finally settled on the "School of International Communism." They worked fast, for within just a couple of minutes they'd finalized the matter. A big-character poster was put up to announce the change, and an official seal was made in no time to finish the procedure. But the new name was quite short-lived because in the end nobody could make out its meaning.

People's names weren't left out of all this. Anyone whose name retained a hint of feudalism should change it immediately, the Red Guards organizations suggested—no, ordered. The trend even bewitched my sister Si Yan and her friends, all of them between eleven and twelve years old. Once, while they were playing at my home, one of them suggested a change because she didn't think her name was revolutionary enough. Every one of them chipped in to suggest new names, trying their best to work out a lofty-sounding one. There had to be "red" in the name, they agreed unanimously. "Red Flower," "Red Heart"—something like that.

My parents looked on with amusement, but when Si Yan asked for permission at the dinner table to change her name to "Red Plum," Father simply told her to finish her meal. She pouted for hours afterwards.

One day, a classmate suggested I change my name.

"It's too soft," he said. Why not change it to a homophone that meant "protect the red sun?" he added.

I'd toyed with the idea of changing my name, but I hadn't seriously considered it before. As it happened, Father forbade it. My name was fine, he said. It meant "blue" and "a feeling of pride and elation." Actually, my name had already been changed once before. I had been given a name from my grandfather, which meant "good at business management." Father wasn't happy with it. It was capitalistic, he said. He beat his brains and leafed through a dictionary until he settled on the current one: Wei Yang. Father was not someone who easily changed his mind. "Don't follow the trend," he said with a contemptuous look, "by changing your name to something like 'rebel.' Before long, all of these people will be changing their names back."

Dahui Temple, a historical site near my home, didn't survive the campaign to "Smash the Four Olds."

A relic of the Ming Dynasty, the temple was several thousand years old. We could see its tiled eaves from the windows of our apartment. Ancient cypress trees encircled the temple walls. They rustled in the breeze, emanating a faint smell from their leaves. Neighborhood children enjoyed going there to play. It was a lovely spot.

One day in September 1966, however, we heard shouting from the loudspeakers on the other side of the wall.

"Down with feudalism, capitalism and revisionism!"

"Smash this feudalist place!"

Red Guards in army uniforms descended on the temple. Before long, a terrifying noise tore through the air. The

Guards were ramming the temple walls with a truck. One of them, standing on a ladder, had reached the head of the Sakyamuni statue. He was hammering out the statue's eyes. Others, including two girls, were destroying the arms of the Thousand-Hand Guanyin.

By the time I got there, two of Guanyin's arms had already fallen to the ground, revealing the unpainted clay inside. As the Red Guards continued, clay and sand kept falling from the ceiling. Scared, I hurriedly went outside. There was a huge plaque above the hall. The Red Guards had tried but failed to pull it down—it was too high for them to reach, even with a ladder, so they turned to something else.

Their eyes fell on a more vulnerable target: a dozen or so painted frescoes on the walls. These paintings told the story of how Guanyin had become a bodhisattva by cultivating herself. The Guards set about defacing the paintings with large brushes. "Down with feudalistic superstition," "Never be bewitched by superstition," and more. Even the arhats lining the walls had been scrawled over with the words "monsters and demons."

They didn't stop there. They began to pull the statue of Sakyamuni onto the ground with a rope. The statue was too big for them, so they did it to an arhat. After tying a rope to its neck, they began to pull with all their might, shouting words to the effect of "We do not fear death, we can pull an arhat down to the ground!" After the arhat crashed to the floor, they hammered the statue into small pieces.

Fortunately, there were no monks living in the temple— otherwise, someone might have been hurt. By the time the Red Guards left, this quiet and historical place had been changed beyond recognition. Debris and clay were everywhere.

✳✳✳

The Summer Palace, too, would soon be "smashed."

This regally-styled garden was not far from my home, just six or seven bus stops away. It was my family's favorite place to visit during weekends. At that time, the Summer Palace had changed its name to the "People's Park in the Capital." One afternoon, my younger sister returned home in high spirits.

"Good news!" she announced. "There will be no more entrance fee charged at the Summer Palace."

That weekend, while my parents were tied up with something, I took my little sister there. The gallery was by Kunming Lake on the southern slope of Longevity Hill. It was a wooden structure 700 meters long, with four pavilions representing the four seasons. The most impressive feature, however, was the gallery of 14,000 paintings on its roof. They were landscapes, flowers and birds, and human characters. We had been there many times before and each time Father would elaborate on the stories illustrated in the paintings.

As soon as my gaze went to the ceiling, I saw it: Many of the paintings had been obliterated. The Red Guards most likely didn't have enough hands to destroy them all because most of the landscapes and flower and bird paintings were still there. But the six or seven thousand paintings of stories from historical or classic novels were gone, erased with thick, ugly coats of white paint. We had a copy of the classic love story *Romance of the Western Chamber* back at home. The gallery used to have illustrations of this story, but no matter how hard I tried, I couldn't see the illustrations. They were gone.

Another favorite story of mine was about the patriotic army general Yue Fei. During the Song Dynasty, he led his troops in fighting off invaders. Before he set off for the battlefield, his mother, in order to encourage him, had written out a phrase on his back with a needle: "Repay the country with utmost loyalty." The painting was still there, but it was now incomplete. The bare-chested Yue Fei could no longer be seen. There was a square of white paint in his place. His mother was lucky, for she still had part of her head visible.

Of all the human figures, only a few from *Journey to the West* were still intact. One of them was the story of how the Monkey King got an upper hand over the Bull Demon King. The paintings may have survived because Chairman Mao had praised the story in one of his poems, lauding the Monkey King's courage in revolting against injustice.

Looking up at the ravaged paintings, my heart sank, but I scolded myself. What was wrong with me? The media spoke highly of the Red Guards. Chairman Mao never said a single word to reproach them. Why was I so confused by their actions? Obviously I had a problem—a big problem. I was no longer a revolutionary. I had to get rid of my sentimentality and sharpen my commitment to the cause.

But no sooner did this thought enter my mind than I remembered Mother's high-heels. All her life Mother had been gentle, generous, and kind to everyone. The only problem with her was her choice in shoes. Was that really a crime? What, I reasoned, was so wrong about Mother's small, simple wish to wear high-heeled shoes? Did the Red Guards really have to suppress such a personal and harmless preference, and what would they smash next?

Until its destruction, the several-thousand-year-old Confucian Temple was a sacred place in past dynasties. Here, its statues are being pulled down.

THE WAR AGAINST CONFUCIUS

Tiananmen Square looked tired the next time I saw it. Forsaken, even. On November 7, 1966, there were no chanting crowds, no fiery speeches. Just a few people milling about the square and several big-character posters flapping against a cold winter sky.

My classmate Xiao Na and I had gotten word that the Red Guards planned to condemn Confucius and his doctrines. Huge numbers of people were expected to turn out, but so far very few people had shown up.

"Where is everyone?" Xiao Na asked.

I shrugged my shoulders.

Xiao Na was a year above me at school. She had large, beautiful eyes and the pale skin of girls from North China. She seemed shy at first, but once I got to know her I discovered that she was actually quite warm and talkative.

I picked up a leaflet from the ground. "A Declaration of War Against Confucius," it read. Like the leaflets printed on our campus, this one was also mimeographed, with a picture of Chairman Mao in profile alongside one of his sayings: "Of all the doctrines of Marxism, revolt is always right!"

Xiao Na and I exchanged looks.

Changes were underway among the Red Guards. Having wreaked havoc in society, some of the original Guards completed their missions only to retreat into history once they fell out of favor with the Party Central Committee's Leading Group for the Cultural Revolution.

Five new leaders emerged: Nie Yuanzi from Peking University, Kuai Dafu from Tsinghua University, Wang Dabin from the Geological Institute, Han Haijing from Beijing Aeronautics University, and Tan Houlan from Beijing Normal University. People had been reluctant to endorse one leader over another, but they believed that by aligning themselves with Madame Mao they couldn't go wrong. The five new Red Guard leaders had outshone others by meeting with Madame Mao and others from the Leading Group. Afterwards they became the mouthpiece of the Group, and anything they did or said was taken as official, to be printed and faithfully followed.

The gathering would be held to the north of the Monument to the People's Heroes. Farther north was the national flag and Tiananmen Tower. By the time Xiao Na and I got there, people from the Normal University had already arrived, shouting, "Down with Confucius Number Two!"

The mass meeting hadn't started yet, and Tan Houlan had yet to appear.

"Why 'Number Two?'" I asked Xiao Na.

"Because he was the second child in the family," she replied. "That's an endearing term within a family, but in this context, it's an insult."

A thought flashed through my mind. "Are they planning on smashing the Temple of Confucius?" I asked.

Pointing toward Tiananmen Tower and then in the direction of the Forbidden City, she answered me with a question of her own. "These two are the greatest symbols of the Four Olds. If they've survived, there must be a reason, right?"

I turned this over in my mind. Once the royal palace for both the Ming and Qing dynasties, the Forbidden City had 9,999 and one-half rooms. Its ornate wooden structures housed the greatest artworks in Chinese architectural history. The Forbidden City topped the list of the five most treasured palaces in the world, ranking higher than the Palace of Versailles, Buckingham Palace, the White House, and the Kremlin. So far the Forbidden City had escaped destruction, but the Red Guards were planning to burn it down. Its rear gate went by the exalted name of "The Gate of Divine Prowess." After New China was founded in 1949, this gate served as the formal entrance to the Palace Museum.

When I first heard that the Red Guards were bent on destroying it, I rushed to the Forbidden City, only to find that the marble plaque bearing the words "The Palace Museum" had been covered up. In its place was a sheet of white paper with words so new they were still dripping with ink: "The Palace of Tears and Blood." A poetic couplet had been pasted to the gate, too. The line on the left read, "Smashing the old world, trample all monarchies and their assistants," and the one on the right read, "Create a new world for the nation." Bisecting these two lines were these words: "Rebellion is always right!" Slogans like "Destroy it!" and "Burn it!" were seen posted on the walls on both sides.

The Forbidden City survived. When the news reached him that Red Guards were coming to burn it down, Premier Zhou Enlai ordered the museum closed and sent a battalion of soldiers to guard it.

But would the Temple of Confucius be lucky, too? I wondered.

Just then a voice rang through the air.

It was Tan Houlan, one of the five new Red Guard leaders. She emerged from the first of several trucks and faced the audience. Short, dark, and bespectacled, she was dressed like a peasant, and it was only after I'd been staring at her for a while that I could tell she was a woman, not a man.

Even with just a small microphone in hand, she proved to be a good speaker, forgoing her prepared speech for an improvised talk. Her voice was hoarse, but her delivery was shot through with emotion. From time to time a strong wind lifted her pigtails. She seemed to me the very incarnation of passion. How could such a small figure hold so much power within her?

Looking out at the crowd, I saw that many people were dressed in army uniforms. I realized I wasn't the only one carried away by her speech. All around me people seemed ready to break the reins that bound them and gallop off into the unknown wilderness.

Voices rose to the song "War Declared on the Reactionary School of Confucianism." Then, facing north to Mao's picture hung on Tiananmen Tower, the two-hundred people Tan Houlan had brought with her read a letter to Chairman Mao. The letter conveyed respect for him, then vowed to destroy Confucius' grave.

"Of all the doctrines of Marxism, rebellion is always right!" the group chorused. With that, six army trucks appeared out of nowhere to whisk Tan Houlan and her men to the railway station.

After the crowd dispersed, I picked up another leaflet from the ground. It was the text of Tan Houlan's speech. The wind had muffled some of her words, but as I read the leaflet I noticed a very passionate and sharp passage. "Here we come," it read. "With the weapon of Mao Thought, we the young people of the Mao era, holding revolutionary banners high, are tracing the footprints of revolutionary martyrs to rebel against the Confucius theoretical school, to smash the two-thousand-year-old den of monsters, the fortress of reactionary forces. It's now or never!"

I was stunned. Confucius' place in the nation's heart was unmatched by anybody, anywhere, and at any time. Born in 479 BC in present-day Shandong province, he was ancient China's greatest thinker, educator, and statesman. He also founded the Confucian School and traditionally retained a stature in China akin to that of Socrates in the West. He stressed compassion, ritual, and duty. Over the past two-thousand years, the nation had regarded him as a sage. His ancestral temple in Qufu drew worshippers from all corners of China, and his former residence was one of the country's largest palaces, just behind those for the Ming and Qing royalties. The temple and residence also held a vast and extremely precious trove of archives and relics.

"We declare war," the leaflet continued, "against the fortress of Confucius; to burn it, to drag its followers off their horses, to shit on the head of their idol. Yes, we are at war with them, with the old world, and nothing will stop us before we achieve victory."

Having read the full text of Tan Houlan's speech, Xiao Na and I exchanged glances.

"Do you really think she'll do it?" I asked.

Looking in the direction of the Forbidden City, she thought for a while before she answered. "They want to make a major statement," she said. "But smashing the Temple of Confucius is an impossible task."

"Why?" I asked.

"China actually has two Confucian temples," she said. "One is in Qufu, Confucius' hometown, and the other in the nation's heart. If Tan Houlan really goes ahead with this plan, she'd face millions of accusing fingers. She'd have to be crazy to do it!"

I thought about this for a moment, and then I said, "But maybe she really has lost her mind?"

★★★

"Absolutely not," Father said when I asked if I could visit Confucius' temple in Qufu. "No one should ever desecrate a grave. The Confucius Temple and the family graveyard?" He shook his head and then pinned me with a look of warning. "You're not going anywhere near there. Don't even think about it, or bad luck will follow you your whole life."

With a visit to Qufu out of the question, my friend Tian Ge suggested another trip to Jinggang Mountain.

"Would you mind if a pretty girl accompanied us?" I asked Tian Ge.

Of course he wouldn't mind.

When I asked Xiao Na if she'd like to come along to Jinggang Mountain, she accepted with a sweet smile.

We were set. I started putting together our itinerary. We had a book of paintings at home called *Beautiful Places of China*. I had long been fascinated by Mount Tai, one of the five most famous mountains in the country. It wasn't far from Beijing, and because transportation was free in those days, I thought we'd stop at Mount Tai before traveling farther south.

But something happened to upset our plans. Halfway up the mountain, we met some Red Guards distributing leaflets claiming that the tomb of Confucius had been blasted open with detonators.

Xiao Na snatched the leaflet from my hand. After a brief glance, she sat down on a roadside rock. She was silent for a long while, her face ashen.

"I want to go see it," she finally said. Her voice was very small.

"You can't go there alone," said Tian Ge, shooting me a look. "We'll go with you."

Father's warning came to mind, and I hesitated.

"No," Xiao Na said when I voiced my worries. "It all depends on our intentions. If we go with good intentions, we'll be safe."

I looked from Tian Ge to Xiao Na.

"Fine," I said, and followed them down the hill to catch a bus.

By the time we arrived, the Temple of Confucius was nothing but a pile of rubble and debris.

On November 15, 1966, two thousand years of Chinese history were swiftly ravaged. Denounced for fostering "bad elements, rightists, monsters, and freaks," Confucius was now an enemy. After a meeting held in front of the temple, where in 1962 a stone tablet was set to designate the place as "a key historic site under protection at the state level," Tan Houlan and her people stormed inside. They smashed and destroyed whatever they could. Exquisite antique paintings, stone tablets, calligraphic works, plaques, and statues—within just a short while, these extremely precious cultural relics were irretrievably lost.

All the statues in the hall had been pulled down and smashed to pieces. Slogans like "Down with. . ." and "Smash the. . ." were pasted all over the walls. The spot originally reserved for Confucius' statue held nothing but shattered rock. The Red Guards, we were told, had tried to pull the statue down so they could parade it through the streets. But the statue was already fragile, and at the first tug of the rope it fell to pieces. Later, the statue's head was affixed onto another one.

Xiao Na lifted her camera to her face and started snapping photograph after photograph. She was silent, pressing the shutter with a trembling finger.

Confucius' tomb was located in his family's ancestral cemetery. The cemetery was one of the three major sites here, the other two being the Temple of Confucius and Confucius' onetime residence. The largest family cemetery in the world, it featured an almost mile-long "sacred path" leading all the way from the Qufu town seat. It was lined on both sides by very tall and very old trees, but by then, the quietness and sacredness of this place was no more. The tombs had been ransacked and broken stone tablets lay scattered in all directions.

Once I had asked Father why the stone tablet was placed on top of a huge stone turtle. It wasn't a turtle, Father corrected, but a legendary animal resembling a turtle. Because turtles enjoyed great longevity, ancient people hoped their names and deeds, like the longevity of turtles, would be passed down through history.

Thinking of my father's words now, I saw that these legendary animals hadn't survived the Red Guards' hammers. All of them had been destroyed.

In the distance I spied two stone tablets still standing. As I walked toward them, I saw two characters freshly painted on the tablets, ostensibly to be kept as records. The Red Guards did it, someone told me, to mark the tablets erected before the Ming Dynasty.

Eventually we found Confucius' tomb. The mound was gone, and in its place was a huge pit.

We learned that when Red Guards and some locals opened the tomb, they found it empty. They registered their anger with a blast, which had left this pit in the ground. Still, nothing was found.

Over the past two-thousand years, Confucius had stood at the foundation of Chinese culture. For generations his graveyard was not to be profaned in any way. It was a crime nobody dared attempt. So how could his tomb be so easily and ruthlessly destroyed now?

Some local people were digging in the dirt, probably trying to find some burial objects. According to an article I read later, one peasant had made a fortune selling relics he found in this place. Dust rose in the distance, but not around the Confucius tomb. It was very quiet. Nobody was around the grave itself, neither local peasants nor the Red Guards.

My schoolmate's lips were tight. Her hands shook as she continued photographing the scene.

"Confucius has two homes and two temples," Xiao Na had told me back in Beijing. Now it struck me: His true home was in the nation's heart, but that heart had turned black.

Something else Xiao Na said when we were on the road came to mind. "Nothing is more sacred in Chinese culture than an ancestral cemetery," she'd said. "It is the root of a person, their eternal home. The worst thing a person can do to another person is to destroy their ancestral cemetery. It is the most vicious insult a family can suffer."

Father's words came to mind once again. As I looked to the site where Confucius was buried, the pit suddenly became a huge eye staring angrily at me.

"Let's go!" I called out to Xiao Na and Tian Ge, waving my arm.

Xiao Na stood up and began walking toward me. Not far from the pit, she suddenly—without warning—began to vomit.

"I can't believe it, I can't believe it," she said over and over on the way back to the county seat. She seemed locked in a trance.

That evening, I found a leaflet from the students of Beijing Normal School. It was a copy of their letter to Mao: "Our respected Chairman Mao: We have revolted. We have pulled the clay statue of Confucius out for public denouncement. The plaque in his residence, the one that read 'guidance forever,' has been removed; Confucius' tomb has been leveled to the ground; the stone tablets praising past monarchies have been smashed, and all the statues in the temple are now gone, their clay removed. . ."

After she left Qufu for home that day, Xiao Na disappeared. I never saw her again. Did she leave Beijing with her family? If so, why did they leave so suddenly? I asked after her more than once, but I never discovered her whereabouts. I didn't forget her, however. I think what we saw at Confucius' grave touched the softest spot of her heart. Xiao Na's disappearance became entangled with my memories of what we'd witnessed together. Many years later, when my eyes fixed on the starry sky, it would sometimes suddenly return to me, the sadness of that day, and I'd send her a silent blessing.

The "Dance of Loyalty" becomes a nationwide phenomenon.

Reading Chairman Mao's quotations was a common practice
before each meal.

RED RITUALS

IN AUGUST 1966, BLOOD BECAME INK.

The Beijing heat was staggering that summer. Classes were suspended, but no formal break had been announced. Students could stay on campus or not—it was suddenly up to them. If you did stay, you camped out in any room you liked. Apart from a brief return home from time to time, I usually stayed on the second floor in the dormitory building for male students.

One day I ducked out of the dorm and saw that a crowd had gathered in front of the school auditorium. Students were reading a freshly issued big-character poster entitled *Red Guards Want to Resist the U.S. in Vietnam*. A passionate composition, it was also a compelling call to action: "We the Red Guards must steel ourselves in braving the rain of bullets in Vietnam by firing real guns at the enemies." The writing style was stirring, but the signatures were downright shocking: Each signature in ink was accompanied by a crimson fingerprint in blood. Several names had been written entirely in blood, with no ink at all.

In Tiananmen Square a month earlier, hundreds of thousands of people gathered to support China in "assisting Vietnam and resisting the U.S." Mao's statement read: "The Chinese people stand behind the Vietnamese in their fight against U.S. imperialism and are ready to meet any need they may have." My classmates were now responding to the call—with signatures inked in blood.

Another question hung in the air. War would prove their valor, but how could they get to Vietnam and who would meet them there when they did? Some male students, perhaps having seen at least a little bit of the world, suggested taking a train to Pingxiang in Guangxi first. The Friendship Pass into Vietnam, Youyiguan, was located there. They claimed they'd pass through without difficulties. Once in Vietnam, the male students would be sent to fight on the front line, while female students would work in hospitals or in propaganda teams. Life would be far more exciting in Vietnam and with a gun in hand.

Sure enough, within two months, four Red Guards from Beijing would manage to sneak across the border into Vietnam. They were determined to join the war and forfeit their lives. This development worried Premier Zhou Enlai. Via telegraph, he relayed the information to the Chinese Ambassador to Vietnam, making it clear that no more students were to join the war. Later it would seem the four students had lost their minds, but at the time, they were considered true revolutionaries and were lauded by many admirers.

*** *** ***

Two days later, a second poster appeared. Again the signatures had been written in blood. Early that morning, the barking of the loudspeakers on campus had awakened everybody. "Shed your blood till the last drop to safeguard Chairman Mao!" The voice called for everyone to add their signatures to the poster.

Rubbing my bleary eyes, I dragged my feet downstairs to do as instructed. By then, big-character posters papered over the entire wall—every day, new ones appeared. I managed to get to the front of the crowd, only to see that the famous *Red Guards Want to Resist the U.S. in Vietnam* poster was barely visible. At its upper right corner was a new poster, *Bombard the Capitalist Headquarters*. Mao had written it himself to encourage the Red Guards to rise up for the Cultural Revolution. Even this poster, however, was partially covered by a brand-new poster with a very long title: *Safeguard Our Great Leader Chairman Mao, Down with the Clique of Liu Shaoqi and Deng Xiaoping, Ready to Shed Blood to the Last Drop!*

The political situation at the time was this: Although regarded as the top two capitalist road-takers, Liu Shaoqi and Deng Xiaoping were still in office. Rumors at my school suggested that Chairman Mao and his Leading Group for the Cultural Revolution were a minority in the central government and the Party Committee as well. Having been promoted by Liu and Deng to their positions, capitalist road-takers were considered accomplices. The Cultural

Revolution, it was presumed, was just beginning to take care of them.

"Truth," the new big-character poster on the wall proclaimed, "is in the hands of the minority!" Chairman Mao presumably fell within that minority. Embroiled in a cruel and relentless power play, Chairman Mao did not merely need the Red Guards to side with him; they had to be willing to sacrifice their lives if needed.

This new poster called upon us to sign in our blood, not ink. I looked around. Several students were cutting their fingers with broken glass or knives. I wanted to do the same—but on second thought, I gave up the idea for fear of infection or pain. I slipped away, hoping no one noticed my lack of courage.

✯✯✯

In terms of both its popularity and the seriousness with which people performed it, the Ritual of the Morning and Evening Reports surpassed all the other Red Rituals.

Nobody knew who invented the form. It certainly hadn't issued from any government decree. Even so, its influence was without parallel—for within just a couple of days, it spread throughout the whole country.

Undertaken with the solemnity of a spiritual observation, the ritual followed a clearly-defined procedure: You would stand before Chairman Mao's picture to ask what you should do and how you should do it during the day. You were supposed to stand before the picture again before you went to bed and report on your activities from the day. This practice was usually conducted in groups, and people sang revolutionary songs to round out the ritual.

People fell into one of two groups—revolutionary or counterrevolutionary. While the first group followed the Red Ritual in the morning and evening, seeking Chairman Mao's instructions about how to conduct their lives, the second group stood before Mao's instructions to do something entirely different—plead guilty. This group wasn't allowed to look squarely at the Great Leader's picture. Actually, they didn't have the right to look at the photograph at all. All they could do was bow in obeisance and pray for forgiveness.

My first exposure to this ritual occurred during a train trip. I was on my way to Shaoshan, the birthplace of Chairman Mao. More than three-hundred people were squashed inside each car. I could barely breathe, much less move, and I'd slept fitfully the night before. As the first rays of sunshine appeared on the distant horizon, I heard someone shout, "It's sunrise, time to make the morning report to Chairman Mao!"

"We can't even stand up!" someone protested. "Let's skip it today."

Objections came from all directions. "We have to do it if we are loyal to the Great Leader!"

"But we can't even stand up properly here," another voice came. "It would be disrespectful if we do it on the floor."

"No," others chimed in, "so long as we are loyal, we can do it even lying on our backs. Now, someone get the *Little Red Book*!"

A heated argument ensued. Somebody shouted, "Stop! We

don't know if the train will even move today. We have no idea where we are. What should we report to the Great Leader, and what instruction can we ask for?"

After a brief silence, a stern, confident voice rose up. "Stop this rubbish! I will beat the pulp out of you if you're disloyal to our leader!"

Whether it was the threat of violence or a sense of guilt that got the upper hand, nobody knew. Anyway, everyone took out their *Little Red Books*.

"First, long live the Great Leader Chairman Mao!" someone began.

Everyone joined in the chorus while raising their hands and holding their books.

"Good health to Vice Chairman Lin Biao—always!"

Now, one by one, people began to address Chairman Mao.

"Please, beloved Chairman Mao," I said, "make the train go faster!"

The person next to me was of a similar mind. "Please, give me something to eat and drink," he said. "We haven't had anything after a whole day on the train, and we've barely covered two-hundred kilometers!"

This wasn't particularly loyal or reverential, I thought to myself, but I wanted exactly the same thing. Amused, I had difficulty hiding my laughter.

On our third morning in the train, as we finished the ritual, we saw a large lake outside the window.

"That's Dongting Lake! We're in Hunan!" someone yelled excitedly. We'd indeed reached Yueyang, and Changsha—

our destination—wasn't far away, and you might have thought from the cheers that the Great Leader himself had conjured the lake for us.

⁂

In the beginning, the Morning and Evening Rituals were simple in content, open to improvisation. But soon they evolved into distinctly different versions. Any deviance from the routine signaled a lack of loyalty. Once, I came across a copy of detailed instructions from a shop's revolutionary committee dated July 19, 1968. It set forth the procedures for Morning and Evening Rituals in exacting detail:

1. Pay respect to the Great Leader Chairman Mao.

The person who leads the ritual: "Our respect to the Great Leader Chairman Mao!" (All stand at attention and echo.)

Everyone rises and salutes Chairman Mao. (Those in hats do a hand-salute, and those who do not, salute with their eyes.) While doing this, they should say in a loud voice, "We remain forever loyal to Chairman Mao."

Leader: Salutation finished.

All: Shout "Long live Chairman Mao" while lowering hands.

2. Longevity to Chairman Mao.

Leader: "Longevity to Chairman Mao, Great Leader of all nations, the red sun in our hearts, our most respected chairman."

All: "Longevity, longevity and longevity!"

Leader: "Good health to Chairman Mao's comrade-in-arms, our most respected Vice Chairman Lin Biao."

All: "Forever healthy, forever healthy!"

3. Sing "The East Is Red."

"Long Live Chairman Mao," "Sailing on the Sea Depends on the Helmsman," or "Chairman Mao is Dearest to Me, Even Before My Parents" may be sung before a morning/evening ritual begins.

4. Make a vow to the Great Leader Chairman Mao.

The leader should recite, followed by all, the "three crucial quotations from Chairman Mao," the first on the first page, the second on the third page, and the second on the seventh page, followed by three new ones: "You should be concerned with state affairs and push the proletarian Cultural Revolution to the end [once]; Do not rest on past achievements, make new ones [twice]; Fight selfishness and revisionism alike [three times]." Other quotations can be recited according to need. Read the first, second and third paragraphs in the foreword from the reprint of the *Little Red Book*.

The leader should say in a loud voice: "Now, make a vow to the Great Leader Chairman Mao."

Everyone: Holding the little red book above the head, "Read Chairman Mao's books, follow his instructions, be a good soldier under his command. We will remain loyal to Chairman Mao, to his great thought and his proletarian revolutionary line." (After this, everyone holds the *Little Red Book* to his/her chest.)

5. Learn instructions from Vice Chairman Lin Biao.

Leader: "Now, recite the inscription Vice Chairman Lin Biao issued to the Navy."

Everyone: "Sailing the seas depends on the helmsman, conducting revolution, on Mao Thought."

6. Leader shouts: "We will follow to the letter the instructions of Chairman Mao and Vice Chairman Lin Biao."

According to the inscription at the end of the document, these procedures had been created by the "revolutionary committee" of a grocery retailer in Lanzhou, Gansu Province. Others gave different (but equally detailed) instructions.

The Morning and Evening Rituals became a simple fact of life, steady and nonnegotiable. Once, a relative of mine with acute appendicitis was told that no surgeon was available to operate on her. "Why not?" she inquired. All the surgeons and nurses were out performing the morning "service." There was no response to her cries, and she had no choice but to wait with her teeth clenched in pain. But that wasn't all. Her procedure exempted her from the Morning Ritual, but she was still obliged to attend the Evening Ritual that day.

One summer evening, when I'd just returned from school for the weekend, I heard Mother laughing.

"That boy will really be somebody when he grows up!" she said to Father.

I seldom saw her laugh in those days, so I asked her what had happened.

"A boy of just five or six in our neighborhood, a little troublemaker," Mother said, "hated napping after lunch. One day his mother came up with a wonderful idea. 'You're a troublemaker,' she said in all seriousness, 'and you should plead guilty to Chairman Mao today.'"

"And what happened then?" I asked.

"The little boy rushed to Chairman Mao's picture and proceeded to plead guilty. He even shed tears! The next day, he napped after lunch every day without protesting. His mother was delighted. 'The ritual is truly magical!' she said to everyone she met."

Afterwards I'd turn this story over and over in my mind. How could a small child be so quickly reformed? It seemed totally improbable. The truth of the story, I finally decided, lay in the mother's faith, for loyalty worked a kind of black magic in those years, and we were all of us thoroughly bewitched.

Red Guards from Hubei Province, a thousand miles from Beijing,
prepare to return home on foot. Before leaving, they pause to honor
Chairman Mao's portrait on the Tiananmen Rostrum.

RED PILGRIMAGE

As an atheist country during the Cultural Revolution, China feared no gods, but in late August 1966 extraordinary numbers of its people set off on pilgrimages.

Unlike pilgrims from elsewhere in the world, those in China were not guided by religious belief but by ideological fervor. All were students, the youngest of them just twelve and thirteen. Their objective was to visit the capital city of Beijing or any other location that had served as a "sacred" revolutionary base during the war years.

Within just a couple of months, more than a hundred-million people were on the road. The authorities didn't classify the phenomena as a pilgrimage, but a *chuan lian*: a journey undertaken to spread revolutionary ideas and to learn from one another. And yet everyone who took part was driven by a conviction no less pious than any religious faith. Mao initiated and supported the undertaking, and to the young pilgrims, he was quite simply a god, the savior of the nation, and his word was sacrosanct.

Because I lived in Beijing, I'd been one of those lucky enough to be received by the savior himself in Tiananmen Square earlier that August. I still longed to make a pilgrimage, however, and I began to set my sights on the countryside.

I'd just turned fourteen, and from the minute I started talking about a pilgrimage, my parents began to fret over my safety. After the Cultural Revolution began, the Red Guards would pass their time on the streets, stopping everyone with long hair or beards, or those with fashionable perms or bellbottoms. These teenagers would "put things right" by giving perpetrators a crew cut regardless of gender, shaving off beards, or snipping off trouser legs with scissors.

"There's so much madness and lawlessness in the city now," Father proclaimed. To prevent me from participating in such activities, he insisted that I stay home and not go anywhere. "No one from the Zhao family will have anything to do with that absurdity!" he said.

Each time I left the house, Father repeated this warning: "Keep in mind your mother's high-heeled shoes." This was still a sore memory for me. Ever since Red Guards accosted her in the streets and Mother limped home barefoot, I hated these kinds of goings-on.

But school was out and I was bored. Father suggested I spend my time studying English. "Don't you want to be a diplomat?" he prodded me. I nodded. "Well, how do you expect to become a diplomat without knowing English?"

I took up my studies, only to let them fall by the wayside.

Distraction was literally next door. Our apartment building was situated among three multi-story buildings.

Some contained dorm rooms and storage rooms belonging to the China Foreign Languages Publishing Bureau (CFLPB). These rooms now housed Red Guards from other parts of the country.

As Chairman Mao's guests, they were extended a warm reception. Word was that the Party's own cooks prepared their meals, and they ate well, with meat, vegetables, and plenty of staples. Their every need was met. Many of these Red Guards were about my age, which made me feel quite envious. Their families' financial constraints might have kept them away, but it had recently been declared that all college students, with the exception of those who were physically unfit or had been to the city before, could now visit Beijing. The privilege was extended to a smaller number of middle-school students—one out of every ten—as well as one out of every hundred faculty members. The government paid for their transportation as well as their room and board. For many young people, this was the opportunity of a lifetime.

I became determined to make a pilgrimage of my own. Father was set against it, but I'd made up my mind. When he allowed my elder brother to travel on foot to Yan'an, a revolutionary base before the founding of New China, I saw an opening.

"As a revolutionary youth," I said one day, steadying my voice, "I should have your support for *chuan lian*, to travel, learn, and spread revolutionary ideas."

At this, Father thought for a while. "Homes are being ransacked and violent fighting is under way in many places," he said at length. "How can a young boy like you stay safe?"

I was silent—my usual rebellious stance in those days.

"Fine," he eventually said. "It will be a learning experience." He then told me he'd long wished to visit Shaoshan in Hunan, the birthplace of Mao. Unfortunately, he hadn't yet had the opportunity. If I liked the idea, why not go and see it in his stead?

I was deliriously happy. Father and Mother began gathering provisions for my trip: a kettle, a traveling satchel, five kilograms of food coupons good for use outside of Beijing, fifteen yuan in *renminbi* cash, plus a blanket. With all this gear, I felt like a millionaire. Fifteen yuan was not a small amount of money in those days. A factory apprentice's salary was about that much. The blanket was a genuine luxury. This was a time when all daily needs were rationed: grain, meat, eggs, and cloth. Each person was allotted just one yard of fabric for the whole year. A blanket cost two cloth coupons, which amounted to two people's annual rations. But apart from its material cost, it was unbounded love and care that my parents had extended to me.

A plan took shape. I would travel with two companions. The first was Tian Ge, my neighbor and friend. One of his parents was my father's colleague. He'd been grounded by his father, too, and like me he'd started rebelling against his parents. Our parents consulted one another and finally agreed to let us travel together. We were joined by another neighbor, Li Xiaohu. He was my schoolmate, but he had much more freedom at home than I did.

The three of us came up with an ambitious plan: First, we would travel to Shaoshan, then to Jinggang Mountain, and then Yan'an—three "holy" places from the revolutionary war period—before we traced the route of the Red Army's

Long March, crossing grasslands and walking over snowy mountains. We were careful to keep this last part of the plan to ourselves.

✯✯✯

With our backpacks full of gear and our hearts full of daring, Tian Ge, Li Xiaohu and I set out one day in late September of 1966.

Years later, I'd see many pilgrims in other parts of the world, but none left as lasting an impression as those I encountered on the Qinghai-Tibet Plateau. Alone and in small groups, they trudged through the snow, their backs against howling winds, prostrating themselves and kowtowing with every step they took, pushing their physical limits to the extremes in their quest to purify their souls.

The scene at the Beijing Railway Station was one of chaos. Red Guards had streamed in from all over the country. After their review before Chairman Mao, some were on their way to the north or south on revolutionary missions. A temporary shed in the square was encircled by red flags and a signboard in front read, "Tickets for Red Guards."

Tian Ge was big—bigger than both Li Xiaohu and me. He led us into the crowd until we found the very end of the queue. Each of us had a letter of introduction from school, which specified our destination and the purpose of our travels. Mine read: "Student Zhao is on his way to Shaoshan, the birthplace of Chairman Mao, to visit and learn. Please give him the necessary assistance for his purpose." The letter was authenticated by a red stamp from the school's revolutionary committee. At that time, the social credit system still functioned and a simple sheet of paper like this was enough to ease our passage. We were lucky— after standing in line for three hours, all three of us received a train ticket heading in the direction of Guangzhou.

If you were to ask me what I thought the most crowded place in all of history had been, I'd immediately say, "The carriages for Red Guards on *chuan lian*." The plaque on the carriage wall read "maximum capacity of 118 people." In fact, several hundred people had managed to crowd inside. Obviously, the railway station had oversold the tickets. With the platform so crowded, the usual way of getting on a train would be impossible. Tian Ge was strongest, so he hopped up into the carriage first. Once inside, he pulled each of us in through a window. We didn't invent this method; other people were doing it and we simply followed suit.

We planned to stick to the spot next to the toilet, but the stream of people pushed us deeper into the train compartment. We were pinned right in the middle. There wasn't a single seat available. I simply sat down on the floor when I needed to rest. I was most amused as I looked around: The tables between each two rows of seats all had people under them, their heads bent low if they were tall. Why had they chosen those spots even though they had boarded earlier than most of the others? I quickly discovered the answer: These people were smart, because when people were packed like sardines in the carriage, they had to remain in a standing position, back to back or face to face. Sitting on the floor was a luxury in such circumstances.

You were in serious trouble when you needed to go to the

toilet. At each stop along the way, the platform became a massive open-air toilet. Some managed to relieve themselves while the train was still moving. Once—by pulling some monkey-like acrobatic moves, holding fast to the overhead luggage shelf and stepping up onto people's shoulders—I managed to get to the toilet, only to see five or six people already inside. Thanks to their kindness, I was able to make my way inside in time. This was why the carriage, even with fairly good ventilation, stank the whole time. But people's enthusiasm for undertaking the Red Pilgrimage was not in the least bit dampened. Hungry, thirsty, and fatigued as we were, one passenger still led the crowd in reciting Chairman Mao's sayings. Someone else directed passengers to sing revolutionary songs.

Before long, we met the first hiccup since setting out. The 1,600-kilometer distance between Beijing and Changsha usually took a train traveling at a normal speed forty hours. But after three days and nights of dawdling on board our train, shifting ahead only sporadically, we'd only managed to reach Hankou. Here the train stood completely still for what seemed like ages. It turned out there wasn't enough coal or water to continue our journey, and we were all told to disembark.

Hankou was an important hub on the route between Beijing and Guangzhou. The huge numbers of people arriving that day pushed the station's capacity to its limit. The food supply was quickly dwindling. After being stranded for three days, we still had no train. We couldn't even obtain a transfer to a train going somewhere else. Unlike in Beijing, getting onto a southbound passenger train here depended on your strength, sheer simian dexterity, and willingness to risk it all. We were just under 200 miles from our destination, but we were unable to move. It was maddening. Our only option was to wait. Each time I heard an incoming train, my heart pounded. I prayed to be able to get on board and continue the journey.

All of a sudden the loudspeakers at the railway station crackled to life. "Due to insufficient carriages, students headed for Beijing to be received by Chairman Mao have priority to leave, while those southbound for Shaoshan will have to take boxcars." A boxcar was a sealed freight container with just two very small openings on either side. After a brief silence came this welcome message from the loudspeaker: "A boxcar is ready to leave for Guangzhou on track number six. It will stop in Changsha."

As if a starter pistol had just gone off, everyone moved, completely disregarding safety as they sprang across the tracks. Luckily, we made it by climbing up into the nearest boxcar. I owed so much to Tian Ge, for after he got on first, he gave each of us a hand to get up, too.

The boxcar was suitable for freight, but for passengers it was a special kind of hell. When the door finally closed, several hundred students were already inside. The darkness inside was not without its benefit, for there was no shyness when answering the call of nature: male students on one side and girls, on the other, relieved themselves through the narrow gap purposely left open at the door.

✷✷✷

Two-and-a-half days later, the train arrived at Changsha. Dislocated train journeys like ours occurred frequently in those days on almost every route that the Red Guards traveled. Like the railways, road transportation was also in total disorder. It became even worse when revolutionaries in the railway industry split into different groups and began battling one another. Some lines simply ceased functioning.

Everyone got off the train at Changsha Station. They were anxious to pay their respects in Shaoshan, the birthplace of Mao. But we three decided to stay in Changsha for a couple of days first, so our immediate priority was to find a reception area for revolutionary students. We found one set up in an auditorium inside a local middle school. Much to my delight, we had rice for our meal there; the rice supply was quite limited back in Beijing. A night's good sleep saw us fully energized the next morning as we headed for the First Normal School of Changsha, where Mao had once been enrolled as a student. Tracing the road he had taken, we soon found ourselves by the Xiangjiang River, which we planned to swim across simply because Mao had done it.

Mao had written a famous poem about this tributary of the Yangtze, and almost everyone at the time knew it. We were told at a very young age how Mao had annealed his physique and willpower by standing in the rain or the fierce sunshine. Sometimes, he made his way from the river all the way up to a hilltop pavilion in the rain. Just two months before, at the age of 73, he had swum across the Yangtze at

Wuhan. "Young people," he encouraged us, "should breast tides and waves by swimming in great rivers."

We were ready now to do as he had suggested. The river water was no longer warm in the early autumn, but nothing could stop us from accomplishing this great mission— swimming across the river as Mao himself had done. Before we got in, we warmed up by reciting "Changsha, Autumn 1925." This was the famous poem Mao had composed about the river, possibly before he dove into the water:

> Standing alone in the ancient autumn,
> Where the Hsiang flows north,
> At the tip of Orange Island,
> Looking over thousands of hills,
> Red all over,
> Stretch upon stretch of woods, all red...

The words perfectly matched the scenery all around us. My sentiments rose as we continued:

> When we were students and young,
> Blooming and brilliant,
> With the emotional discourse of young intellectuals,
> Fists up, fists down,
> Fingers pointing at the river and mountain,
> Writing, full of excitement,
> The lords of a thousand houses mere dung!

My emotions welled up as we came to the end:

Remember still,
How, in the middle of the stream,
We struck the water,
Making waves which stopped
The running boats?

The river was cold but very clear. We carefully sealed the plastic bags with everything we had in them and then we jumped into the water in just our underwear. The river was narrower in the autumn than in the spring and summer, and we could see straight down to the riverbed.

"Don't rush," Tian Ge said, taking on the voice of an elder brother, "just keep a steady pace. Otherwise you may get a cramp in your calves."

The weather was nice that day, the water calm and smooth. Before long, we reached Orange Beach in the middle of the river, where we didn't even stop for a break, but continued on until we got to the shore on the other side. The moment I stepped out of the water I shuddered and began hopping from one leg to the other to keep warm.

We weren't the only ones performing this ritual. In the distance several other people were swimming in the river, too. We watched them for a while and then fell back into conversation. All of a sudden, Tian Ge leapt into the river, and we realized that a girl was struggling in the water. Tian Ge and another young man hauled her back onto the riverbank. After thanking Tian Ge profusely, she tossed her hair to the side, puffed out her chest, and announced, "Didn't Chairman Mao say, 'Be resolute, fear no sacrifice, and surmount every difficulty to win victory'? Well, thanks to these two, I've done it!"

Despite the frigid temperature, we planned to continue up to Mount Yuelu in our underwear without even drying off. But rescuing the girl had cost us time, and the cold weather was proving a bit too much for us, so at Tian Ge's suggestion we canceled the mountain-climbing part of our pilgrimage. Even so, we felt proud, revitalized by our newfound strength and stamina.

Changsha was only sixty miles from our destination of Shaoshan. There was a bus heading that way, but to make up for the disappointment of not hiking up to Mount Yuelu after the crossing, Tian Ge suggested we go there on foot. Li Xiaohu and I readily agreed.

Hunan Province was hilly and picturesque. We never felt lonely on the road because there were many pilgrims traveling in the same direction. They came from all over the country, even distant Inner Mongolia and the Northeast. In those days, Red Guards on the road were quite a sight. Most of them wore army uniforms and traveled in groups ranging from half a dozen to a dozen people. Usually, the Red Guard in front carried a picture of Chairman Mao. This was most often a color print of a famous oil painting of the Chairman in which he was shown on his way to Anyuan to meet mine workers. In the painting, Mao is dressed in a long gown holding an umbrella. Dark clouds hover over the mountains behind him, suggesting the difficulties of the past. In the eyes of later artists, the brushing technique of this painting was far from perfect, but at the time it was regarded as an artistic treasure. The painting also had a legendary print-run of more than 900 million copies.

Some Red Guards also designated someone to lead with a red banner bearing the name of their organization. From time to time, the melodies of revolutionary songs rose into the air. Sometimes, they recited Mao's sayings in unison. "Be resolute," went the most often-recited one, "fear no sacrifice and surmount every difficulty to achieve victory!"

Two-and-a-half days later, we found ourselves in the small village of Shaoshan.

Our letters of introduction clearly made a big difference. Because we had come from Beijing, instead of staying in a villager's home we were sent to spend the night in a local auditorium. All the seats had been removed from the auditorium, and the floor was covered with bamboo mattresses on top of thick straw. Dozens of students had slept there before us. The mood inside was celebratory. Deep into the night, the loud recitation of Chairman Mao's poems and sayings went on and on until sometime near dawn everyone finally fell into an exhausted sleep.

The next morning, locals guided us to Mao's former residence. There was a long line in the front, more than a mile long, and it never seemed to get any shorter. Once people in the front finished their visit and left, newcomers arrived to line up at the end. Everyone moved in silence and with the most sincere esteem.

I walked slowly through every room in the house—its guestroom, bedrooms, and kitchen. I wanted to commit every detail to memory. There were a few pieces of very simple furniture and some farming tools. Simple and common as they were, they had once belonged to Mao and they were sacred items now.

I lingered in Mao's bedroom longer than in any other room in the house. The bed differed from those found in the north, with poles at each corner holding up a mosquito net. Next to the bed was a long table; this likely had been Chairman Mao's desk. I tried my best to imagine Mao as a young boy in this room. I scanned the ground, hoping to discover some straw, a hoe washed clean after use, or—even better—footprints, but I saw none of these. Obviously the place had long since been thoroughly cleaned and tidied.

Following the crowd, I treaded a path around a small hill for a couple of minutes, where I found myself at the graves of Mao's parents. There were just two simple earthen mounds with a stone tablet above them. Dozens of incense sticks stood burning in front of the graves. Dozens of Red Guards were kowtowing on their knees and chanting: "My respect to Chairman Mao's parents!" and "Long live Chairman Mao!"

I didn't like kowtowing, so I purposely dropped back from the crowd. When everybody had passed me, I stopped to observe the surroundings, hoping to find something unusual about this place. China has a long history of geomantic theory, about which I knew nothing at all, but I had once read a book about the geomantic omens found in Mao's birthplace. Incredibly, it was a publication of the Party Literature Research Center of the CCP Central Committee. According to the book, a mysterious sign appeared the night before Mao's birth. His mother saw a dragon standing in front of their family temple and a fire behind the house on the hill, while his father also saw in his dream a martial-looking general clad in armor appearing at their doorway. When asked why he was there, the general simply said, "By the instruction of the Heavenly King, I have come to guard your house." It sounded quite superstitious, but given the publisher, nobody ever doubted the truthfulness of the story.

Standing here now, no matter how hard I tried, I failed to see anything extraordinary in the view. Yes, the scenery and fresh air were lovely, but they didn't strike me as exceptional. In the end, I just breathed in deeply, hoping to store up the energy of this place in my lungs.

Afterwards I felt guilty for failing to show my respect by kowtowing to the graves of Mao's parents. I suggested walking back to Changsha as a way to redeem ourselves. Tian Ge and Li Xiaohu shot me an odd look, but they agreed to go with me.

It was a foolhardy decision and in the end I got what I deserved, for halfway along the road, I nearly collapsed. The cold was bone-splitting and I had no strength left in me. Before long, an army truck stopped and some soldiers asked if we needed help. They could give us a ride, they said. Obviously, my shaky steps had caught their attention. Tian Ge and Li Xiaohu quickly hopped inside the truck, but I declined the kind offer. Brimming with pride and youthful conviction, I hobbled all the way back to Changsha by myself.

ON JINGGANG MOUNTAIN

THE JINGGANG MOUNTAINS LIE IN THE MIDDLE SECTION OF the Luoxiao mountain chain in Ji'an County, south of Nanchang. Covering a distance of nearly 260 square miles, the forested mountains, with their rolling peaks and winding streams and rivers, hold a special place in the history of the Chinese Revolution. It was here that Mao, Zhu De and Peng Dehuai met in October 1927 to found a revolutionary base. In the beginning, they were a very small force, armed with only spears and broadswords. At the time nobody expected that this small group of men, a mere spark of fire, would be able to ignite a flame that would sweep across the whole of China.

Now, four decades later, people were trekking to Mao's former base camp from all over the country to pay their respects. I came to understand years later that we pilgrims were nothing but pieces on a political chessboard. No matter how pious or smart we thought we were, we were in the hands of the chess player—or, to put it another way, we'd all been positioned and manipulated for a political purpose.

This was actually no secret. When asked the reason for Mao's endorsement of the pilgrims, Chen Boda, the head of the Party's Cultural Revolution Leading Group, explained, "their travels can bring revolutionary experience to other parts of the country, making it possible for Red Guards to compare notes, to see who is really revolutionary and who is not, and who are Chairman Mao's genuine followers and what the true purpose of proletarian headquarters is." This statement, approved by Chairman Mao, asserted that the Red Guards and their *chuan lian* were necessary to light the fire of revolution; it was one of the great strategic inventions of the Cultural Revolution.

The speech became widely known. Numerous pamphlets were printed and reprinted by school newspapers. By that time, I had returned from Shaoshan. As a student reporter for our school newspaper *Jinggangshan*, I was thrilled, and very much honored, to have made a pilgrimage there. Still, I felt I needed to undertake another trip to prove myself.

Not long afterwards, I set off for the Jianggang Mountains with my friend, Tian Ge, wholly ignorant of the trauma awaiting me there.

☆☆☆

It was snowing when Tian Ge and I arrived on the mountainside. With all the transportation systems down, our only choice was to hike up the mountain and stay in a shed for the night. Unlike Shaoshan, Jinggang Mountain had many sites available for pilgrims to pay their respects to Chairman Mao: the martyrs' mausoleum, a museum, Mao's former residence, and Huangyangjie, famous as a place where the weak defeated the strong in battle.

Having visited all of these sites, we were ready to leave, but then the incredible news came that Chairman Mao was coming to greet the Red Guards at Jinggang Mountain.

This news came by way of pamphlets printed by the Red Guards. Even the time, the place, and the people who would be present were specified. Tian Ge and I were thrilled—what an honor to be received by our "god" in this holy place! It was the opportunity of a lifetime. How could we possibly miss it?

Overnight the mountain became magnetic. Those who had already come refused to leave, while even more Red Guards arrived. People who were already down the mountain, waiting for transportation, now came back on foot. All the schools in the neighboring provinces were deserted; the students had all set off for Jinggang Mountain.

This was more than the local authorities could handle. The loudspeakers at every reception area insisted that Chairman Mao was not coming. It was no use. This three-square-kilometer area was already packed with people. Nobody was leaving, and more kept coming.

Putting up so many people for the night presented an enormous problem. All the lodgings were over their maximum capacity, and so were the classrooms of the local primary and middle schools and the family dwellings of the peasants. Even the huts that the local government had put up in haste were full. Ice was shoveled away and then tents were put up in the mud. It still wasn't enough. To keep warm, latecomers spent the whole night standing around a bonfire.

We were lucky, for we had a little space in a shed. But this was a blessing in disguise. Due to the overcrowding, all reception areas came up with a rule—lodging would be provided to each Red Guard for just two days, after which their cotton-padded quilts would be retrieved and then given to others. To prolong our stay—and the possession of our quilts—Tian Ge and I pretended to be ill or simply wrapped ourselves in the quilts as we walked around.

"Great knowledge lies in travel and reading," Chinese people say. My trip to Jinggang Mountain proved the truth of that saying. I saw how tenacious you had to be to survive in that place. On a very steep and zigzagging mountain path, with irregular steps that stretched ever onwards, I saw a peasant carrying a shoulder pole with loads on each end. While we were panting and sweating all over, I saw steam rising from his head, but each step he took forward was firm.

I saw something very surprising one snowy night. Exhausted and hungry, we spied an earthen hut ahead with a light on inside. We knocked at the door, and a peasant opened it. He invited us in, asking if we were hungry and needed food. The hut was totally bare. Neither Tian Ge nor I had the heart to trouble the peasant. We declined his kind offer of food and lay down on the ground to sleep. Then, just before closing my eyes, I noticed a picture of Liu Shaoqi on the wall.

By this time, Liu Shaoqi had been overthrown. Why was his picture still here, proudly displayed on a wall inside the hut of a local peasant, in this cradle of revolution? I was confused. There had to have been other Red Guards staying in this place. Hadn't anyone kindly admonished this peasant of his gaffe?

The next morning, as we proceeded up the mountain, a huge live oak in Huangyangjie rose up before us, tall and in full leaf. Its foliage was like a gigantic umbrella. Not far from the local people, the Red Army led by Mao and Zhu De had rested under it each time they shipped grain from outside the mountain. When I saw it, all the leaves within reach were gone. They had become souvenirs for the Red Guards. In their place were a multitude of red armbands. From a distance they looked like burning flames on the bare branches.

Two Red Guards were vying to hang their armbands on a higher branch. The higher they were, the more revolutionary they believed they were. A slogan I'd seen a couple of days before came to mind: "Zhu De was a warlord!" It was right on the panel of the local museum, and it must have been there for a long time. Obviously, nobody had bothered to point out its absurdity. My mind, once again, was confused.

What most impressed me on this trip was a small lamp I saw in Bajiaolou. Somehow my heart itself seemed illuminated by it. There was nothing special about it—just an eight-inch-tall bamboo tube, on top of which was an iron spoon with lamp oil and a wick. The lamp sat on top of a small wooden table by Mao's bed. I knew the years he'd lived in this place had been extremely difficult years, but Mao had kept up his confidence and courage. It was here, by the light of this same lamp, that Mao wrote what would become the famous tract, "Why Is It That Red Political Power Can Exist in China?"

My imagination was suddenly galloping ahead of my thoughts. It dawned on me that the aspiration of just one person could change the course of history. At that moment, I felt as if the lamp had been turned on. In my mind's eye, it was bright enough to light up the whole mountain.

Of course it was just an illusion. At that time, the mountain was still snow-capped. The weather was very cold. But nothing could dampen the enthusiasm of the Red Guards who came to this place. It was common knowledge that this mountain held a special position in Chairman Mao's heart. Back in 1959, at the Lushan Conference, he'd made a famous remark: "If the People's Liberation Army refuses to go with me, I will go back to Jianggang Mountain, where I'm sure I can find the Red Army." One year before the Cultural Revolution, while in his seventies, he did go back. This was the place where he would write, "Nothing is too difficult if you put your heart to it."

Well, that was history. Now, with more and more Red Guards on their way, more than 200,000 people were crowded into one square mile. Food and lodging were becoming critically scarce. Worse still, without medical care, diseases such as fever, colds, and diarrhea were setting in. An epidemic was not impossible.

When eventually helicopters arrived to air-drop food and medicine onto the mountain, they would bring a different tragedy.

✦✦✦

"Chairman Mao is coming to greet you today!"

A Red Guard rushed into our hut with this fantastic piece of news. Before we could ask him any questions, he disappeared outside to spread the news. Tian Ge and I sprang to our feet. Outside our hut, Tian Ge and I saw the whole valley exploding with excitement. "Long Live Chairman Mao!" was heard nonstop, and people were running about like mad in all directions.

Looking across the mountainside, I began to worry: Where was Chairman Mao going to receive us? There didn't seem to be any flat space large enough for that. There was no structure there like Tiananmen Tower.

Tian Ge thought he had the answer. "Come with me," he whispered. While we were walking down a slope, he explained his theory. "The roads are covered in snow. There's no way cars can get up here. Chairman Mao must be taking a helicopter and the best place for landing is that flat space over there."

I looked in the direction he was pointing. He was right. A patch of snowy ground had just been plowed, and PLA soldiers were standing guard nearby. There were others who were just as smart, though, for many others had already arrived to find the best vantages around the presumed landing area. Following Tian Ge, I squeezed into the crowd to stand next to a guard.

The soldiers seemed to confirm what we'd heard. More people were coming this way. My eyes were fixed on the dark clouds above us, ears listening attentively for the sound of a motor. It was still very cold. Many people didn't have heavy coats, but none of them left. Nobody wanted to miss this historic moment. Every face was written over with piousness. The cold was irrelevant. The piercing wind was irrelevant. Actually, nothing else was relevant at all. Everyone was standing, anxiously waiting for a miracle to happen.

And then there it was! A dark dot in the distant sky, coming closer and closer.

It was a helicopter with an army emblem painted on its fuselage. People burst out, "Long live Chairman Mao!" Everyone began to push to the front. I was nearly swept off balance into a nearby dung pit. But the dutiful army guards, arm in arm, formed a tight ring that was impossible to penetrate.

The helicopter didn't land immediately, but circled a couple of times as if the great man on board was looking down on the populace. The helicopter descended, attempting to land—but each time it tried it pulled up again, as if not wanting to scare anyone below. Finally, it landed in a very gentle manner, even though the strong current of air from its rotors knocked off all the ice on the nearby tree branches.

Someone cried out in alarm. Chairman Mao had indeed come. Anxiety seized the crowd. How desperately they wanted to see Chairman Mao in person! Before the helicopter came to a complete standstill, before the propellers stopped, the crowd could no longer contain itself. A human tide burst forward, butting the ring that the army men had formed. Like a leaf in a wave, I was swept this way and that. And then a tragedy occurred.

Two Red Guards broke the ring and surged forward. One of them, just fifteen or sixteen years old, shouted to someone at the back. I couldn't understand what he said, because he was speaking in his home dialect. It was the Ningbo dialect, someone told me later—the most difficult-to-understand of all dialects in China. "I want to be the first to shake hands with Chairman Mao!" he shouted.

He never did, for just seven or eight meters forward, he seemed held up by some invisible force, possibly from the force of the rotors that were still spinning around. He tried to wrestle himself free, but it was too late. A blade chopped his head in half. A thick liquid of red and white burst outward from his neck.

I was aghast. Was this some nightmare? I screwed my eyes shut and then opened them again.

Now the blades had stopped completely. There was dead silence.

Probably half a minute later, the dead man's companion realized what had happened. He went up to the liquid on the ground. He picked up a little with his hand, which he tried to shovel back into the dead man's skull, as if in that way he could bring his companion back to life.

Not a sound was heard in the valley.

After what felt like ages, the door of the helicopter opened. All eyes lifted, ready to meet the Great Leader.

But it was not Chairman Mao who appeared—just a few soldiers with some boxes of medicine. Nothing more.

✯✯✯

An emblem of the Cultural Revolution, to this day Jinggang Mountain receives visitors every day. But their purpose is different. The place is no longer a holy site for a "red pilgrimage," but a "tourist destination."

I left Jinggang Mountain with mixed feelings. My mind was even more confused than when I'd first set out on my pilgrimage. Back home, my thoughts began to unravel and shift. The image of the man and his severed head were seared in my mind. And then, with time, my zeal began to fall away, and I lost interest in nearly everything.

WAR OF THE REBELS

THE NEWS HIT BEIJING ON NEW YEARS' DAY, 1967: TWO rebel groups in Shanghai had clashed violently.

Beijing was shrouded in dark clouds. Northwesterly winds had brought a bone-chilling cold. As usual, I woke with a start to the sound of the loudspeakers from across the street on the campus of the Central Academy of National Minorities. This morning it was an editorial from the *People's Daily* for New Year's Day entitled "Push the Proletarian Cultural Revolution to the End." The article asserted that "the year 1967 will be one of class struggle across the country, the year of an all-round attack on class enemies."

With so many high-ranking government officials and army officers struck down over the previous few months, the government had largely stopped functioning. I was confused by the fact that classes were no longer being offered at my school. What about my education? With so much chaos, where was the country headed? Would these latest events affect my father? As the head of the Spanish-language section of the *Beijing Review*, a magazine published by the Chinese Foreign Languages Publishing Bureau (CFLPB), he'd already had a hard time. He'd been removed from his post under suspicion of spying for the U.S. government simply because he'd studied there as a young man. Demoted from his position, he was now working as a typist in his department. I wasn't worried about him losing his job, but the possibility of his being taken away for another round of background checks terrified me. His career would be doomed, and so would my own prospects.

Father was worried, too, but to relieve our fears, he behaved as if nothing bad could happen. After he returned home from work, he would cheerfully tell us how much progress he'd made that day. But my heart was always heavy—very heavy.

✷✷✷

"We'll finally be eating meat today!" Mother announced one morning.

She reached into her purse and produced the only two food coupons we had left, then asked me to go stand in line for this rare treat. Material supplies were quite limited in those years, and almost everything was rationed out with coupons.

My sister Si Yan was too young to figure out that something might be up. She simply clapped her hands in great excitement and said cheerfully: "We're going to have meat today! Meat, meat, meat!" She asked if she could go along with me, so the two of us walked to the nearest grocery store and returned with half a pound of pork. For the first time in months, Mother smiled. At lunchtime, she emerged from the kitchen with a plateful of stir-fried pork slices and Chinese cabbage. I was busy helping myself to the food when an old woman shouted from downstairs, "Telephone call for Zhao Weiyang from Apartment 202!"

I rushed down to the reception room, where the only telephone for the neighborhood was installed. The call was from Wang Zhigang, a senior schoolmate and deputy chief editor of the campus newspaper *Jinggangshan*.

"We're publishing an extra feature," he said excitedly. "We need you to help with the stencil paper for printing."

"What's the feature about?" I asked.

"Big news!" he said. "Something's happened in Shanghai. Some rebel groups there got physical, using anything they could lay their hands on to fight each other! A hundred-thousand people were involved, the first time ever in this country!"

A hundred-thousand people fighting one another on the streets? It was an almost unimaginable scene.

There was no way for people to stay out of the Cultural Revolution. They generally fell into one of two groups: rebels or conservatives. Both followed the mantra "rebellion is always right," and they both claimed allegiance to Chairman Mao and his revolutionary line. Red Guards also fell into two factions. Those who emerged early were the conservatives, made up of students from high-ranking officials' families. To them the phrase "like father like son" was implicitly true; they were unwilling to surrender the benefits that their parents' generation had enjoyed.

Student Red Guards on either side had completed their mission. Their time was over now. They no longer stood under the Cultural Revolution's stage lights, nor did the Leading Group of the Cultural Revolution hold them in favor any longer. Rebel groups from factories and other sectors of society had taken their place.

I shoved aside the delectable plate of pork and lost no time rushing to school. The student paper was located in a classroom equipped with special colored paper and tools for mimeographing. The title of the forthcoming feature, Wang Zhigang instructed, had to be very bold, very eye-catching. He handed me the story. "The Incident on Shanghai's Kangping Road," it read. Did he write it himself, or had he copied it from somewhere? There was no way of knowing.

Kangping Road was famous. The CCP Shanghai Committee was located there. Those who sided with the municipal government were called "conservatives" and those rising up against it were called "rebels." The conservatives, who sided with the local government, had a team of around 800,000 factory workers. They were formally known as the "Workers' Red Guards of Mao Thought in Shanghai." They were, however, on the losing side of the battle. Their opponents, the "General Headquarters of Shanghai Revolutionary Workers"—the "Workers' Headquarters" for short—were the rebels. Conflicts between the two sides had been raging for a long time, but the tensions had recently escalated into fighting. After setting up an office in the famous Hengshan Hotel, the rebels enlisted 100,000 people to attack a municipal government building which then served as the conservatives' headquarters. After enduring waves of punching, kicking, and bludgeoning, 20,000 conservatives were captured. The next morning, they slowly moved in six rows to a designated spot. All of their armbands were stripped off and piled up in the yard.

Ninety-one conservatives were hospitalized. This was the first armed conflict to occur since the beginning of the Cultural Revolution. It was also a turning point in the way the Cultural Revolution was conducted. As a result of this battle, the rebel faction took power over the Shanghai government and the CCP Shanghai Committee. Former leaders Chen Pixian and Cao Diqiu were shooed out of office.

Chairman Mao approved of the takeover. To him, this was the right way to transform the government's power structure on all levels. "When the revolutionary forces unite in Shanghai," he said, "everywhere else, including the eastern part of China, will follow, and the whole country will have hope." *Red Banner*, the mouthpiece of the CCP, called on other parts of the country to do the same. Things didn't stop there. Several days later, the Leading Group of the Cultural Revolution lauded the takeover in Shanghai in a telegram that read: "Your revolutionary act has set a brilliant example for all factory workers and revolutionary people in the country." This was the "January Storm," an event no less momentous than the October Revolution in Russia.

This "January Storm" did set an example for the rest of the country, but it was an example of how to seize power with violence. Rebels in different parts of the country followed suit. Once violence occurred, more would follow. It was the principle of inertia. At the beginning, the violence was limited to bludgeoning, but with an escalation of intensity, firearms from the military arsenal were somehow released—first accidently, and then deliberately. So the weapons changed. Bludgeons were replaced by rifles, machine guns, and grenades—even tanks were seen from time to time on the streets. Things were out of control. Chaos prevailed. Cities and villages now became battlegrounds for guerrilla war.

★★★

My school was not spared from the "January Storm." By that time, after repeated instruction from the Party Central Committee, the practice of sending Red Guards across the country to spread revolutionary ideas had ended, and young people had returned to school. But with no classes being offered, what were they supposed to do? Undertake revolution? How? Seize power like others were doing across the country? That was out of the question, so the students directed their attention to the school's administration.

The Red Guards in my school fell into three groups. All of them refused to back down, all of them wanted power over the school, and all of them had loudspeakers installed at various buildings on campus. They accused each other of taking "capitalist and reactionary lines," urging their members to switch sides.

I had no interest in these squabbles. I stayed home most

of the time after the Chinese New Year and I'd become something of an idler. Much to my delight, my English studies had seen rapid progress—thanks to the help from Father. The crystal radio I'd constructed was working fine, providing me with clear reception. My calligraphy improved, possibly from repeatedly cutting wax paper for *Jinggangshan*.

Still, I returned to school from time to time for short periods. This was to fend off any accusations from others.

By then, the old room assignments for the dorms had long since been discarded, but I chose to stay in my original room. My dormitory building, located on the eastern side of the campus, faced the Fragrant Hills Institute for Orphans, with just a paddy field in between. The building had been transformed from an original classroom block. Desks and seats had been replaced by bunk beds. Stairs in the middle of the corridor led to the top floor. With the intensive sparring taking place on campus, this building took on a new function: the third and fourth floor became the headquarters and fortress of the Red Guards of Maoism, while the first and second floor didn't change, and still functioned as dormitories for male students.

One night in April or May—I can't remember which—the loudspeakers of the Maoism group and the Red Flag Corps had stopped their routine daylong accusations against each other. All of us, or nearly all of us, were safely in bed when a great bang suddenly sounded from next door. A number of us rushed over to take a look.

A window had been smashed. Broken glass lay in shards on the ground. The "culprit" was soon discovered—half a red brick lying on one of the bed's, having accomplished its mission. The bed's occupant, a slight, bespectacled boy, was still in shock, his eyes fixed on the corner of the wall. Others had sprung out of bed and were now dressing in haste. One cursed angrily, "Son of a bitch, can't they even aim? This is only the second floor!" But before he could finish his sentence, another bang sounded. It sounded like the exterior of the wall was being rammed. "Get away from the window!" someone cried out. "It's a slingshot from the Red Flag Corps!"

The cause was quickly established—retaliation for an assault that the Red Flag Corps inside the opposite building had suffered at the hands of the Maoism faction earlier that morning. The culprits had proved themselves poor marksmen; the second floor of our building had been struck unintentionally.

I was worried. My bed and I could also end up victims to this little skirmish. As a fifteen-year-old, however, curiosity took the upper hand. Maoism was based in this building, I realized—and to my knowledge, they too had similar catapults capable of firing bricks. I followed two male students up to the roof, where I saw much confusion among the Maoism people. Some were shouting angrily, "Fire back, fire back!" Their arsenal contained bludgeons and iron tubes cut to sharp tips.

Obviously they were poorly prepared for this attack. Some of them were throwing bricks, while others were making a giant catapult. A single bed was left upside down, with bicycle tires fixed onto the legs as rubber bands. There were other beds in the same position. Before I approached for a closer look, one of them shouted at me: "You're not one of us! Join us or piss off and never come back to this building!" I quickly retreated. Before I was back on the second floor, desks and chairs had already been thrown down from the roof, blocking the stairwells.

★★★

Early the next morning, I took the first bus back to my parents' apartment. When I got home, I expressed my doubts as I spoke to my father. I said that I was confused by what was happening at school. He was silent for a moment, and then he admitted he was unable to understand what Chairman Mao and the Leading Group of the Cultural Revolution were thinking just now.

"No matter what other people do or say," he cautioned me, "life is a one-time-only event, and it deserves to be treasured and respected."

I leafed through the *People's Daily* newspaper over the next few days. I could see that the "January Storm" was raging. Rebels in different provinces were fighting—yes, literally fighting with weapons. Everybody wanted power.

Shanxi Province was the first after Shanghai. On January 14, 1967, in their "Announcement Number One," the Shanxi Revolutionary and Rebellion Headquarters made their intentions very clear: "The takeover becomes effective from this day, and all power that the CCP Shanxi Committee used to hold is now ours." A few days later I learned that they had the support of the Leading Group of the Cultural Revolution behind them. The *People's Daily* lauded their actions, stating: "The takeover by Shanxi revolutionaries was justified, a fine example set for proletarian revolutionary rebels across the country."

Next came Guizhou Province. On January 25, the Guizhou Proletarian Revolutionary Rebels' General Headquarters announced: "Our takeover of all power from the provincial government and the Party Guizhou committee is accomplished, including power over politics, finance, administration, everything. It is effective from today."

Heilongjiang Province outshined the others with its "Red Rebels from the Harbin Military Industry," a body that Mao Yuanxin, Mao's nephew, had founded. With support from Mao's nephew, the Party secretary of the Heilongjiang Committee, Pan Fusheng, announced the founding of the "Heilongjiang's Red Rebels' Revolutionary Committee." For a time, it was even called the leading organization of the province, said to be the first leading body with "revolutionary committee" in its name. Two days later, an editorial in the *People's Daily* sang its praises, describing the Heilongjiang example as very original.

This revolutionary committee was a three-in-one body made up of representatives from various local revolutionary groups, the local People's Liberation Army, and former government workers. Two months later, *Red Banner*, another Party mouthpiece, published Mao's latest instruction: "Any place or working unit that needs to be taken over should have new authorities. Even temporarily, these authorities must be revolutionary, proletarian, and highly representative. Their name? 'Revolutionary committee' should be appropriate." Credit for this mode of power acquisition went to Heilongjiang Province. Many other places followed suit.

But the takeover was met with resistance in some places. Even the instruction from Mao failed to take effect. The three-in-one practice didn't work everywhere, or if it did, it became instrumental in power struggles. Every group wanted a slice of the pie. When word of mouth failed to serve their purposes, armed fighting broke out, and once the fighting started, the bloodshed would be devastating.

IN THE REVOLUTIONARY FASHION

ALL ACROSS CHINA, CHAIRMAN MAO'S LIKENESS HAD BECOME a fashion craze. I bought my first Chairman Mao badge from a department store near my school. I had to stand in line for ages to fork over ten fen. It was a luxury in a time of few adornments. My new badge depicted Mao's face in relief from the side, gold on enamel red. I liked it very much, particularly when I wore it pinned to my four-pocket blue coat. A song had even been composed for when you wore this accessory, and I now belted it out with joy:

> I have Chairman Mao's badge on my chest,
> On my chest,
>
> It shines with golden rays,
> The red sun swells from my heart,
>
> From my heart!

By wearing a badge like this, you showed your deep devotion. Some people even stabbed the pin through their skin and their flesh, hoping to outdo others in their loyalty. They let the blood flow for others to see. To them, this was one way to make the badge and their bodies converge into one.

New styles emerged. Some bore Chairman Mao's profile and his calligraphy, or a revolutionary base during the war years, paired with lines resembling plums, pines, bamboo, the sun, stars, or the moon. Some were round in shape, others oval or heart-shaped; some were fashioned from aluminum, others with silver, crystal, plastic, organic glass, or porcelain. The size got bigger and bigger, some reaching twenty centimeters in diameter and wearable only with a silk ribbon hung around the neck. Some estimates suggest that there were more than ten thousand varieties.

Many factories discontinued making their other products in favor of badges. Even the aircraft industry suffered, for too much aluminum was going into badges. Chairman Mao eventually intervened with a special instruction: "Give airplane manufacturing back to me." Even so, new varieties kept coming out.

✵✵✵

Revolutionary zeal next took the shape of a dance. The so-called "Dance of Loyalty" consisted of simple moves that were easy to learn, regardless of age or gender, but capable of conveying a strong political message. By late

1966, men and women, old and young, were dancing anytime and anywhere.

I'd mastered the steps before the 1966 National Day. A mass parade was scheduled in Tiananmen Square to celebrate the 17th National Day of the People's Republic of China. At the time, the population of Beijing was about six million. Of those, one-and-a-half million people were expected to attend; almost a third of them were Red Guards from other parts of the country. Beijing itself still needed to provide more than a million attendees, about one-fifth of the city's population. It would be the largest parade in the nation's history.

My classmates and I were ordered to take part. To us, there was no greater honor. We would pass Tiananmen Tower in a quick and orderly fashion while Chairman Mao waved to us from the tower. We would festively sing and dance. Like other schools, ours had a propaganda team for Mao Thought, and it was made up of girls who were good at singing and dancing. To better prepare us, they came to tutor us in the Dance of Loyalty.

Singing was one of my favorite activities, but I was a clumsy dancer. The tutors who arrived to teach us, however, were sweet, pretty, and young. That was enough to encourage me to work hard to learn the dance. We practiced "The Respected Chairman Mao," a song I had learned long before then. Its lyrics went:

> The respected Chairman Mao,
> You are the red sun in our hearts.

We have so many things to tell you.
We have so many songs to sing for you.

Millions of red hearts are poured out to you.
Millions of faces are smiling to the red sun.

Long live the Great Leader Chairman Mao;
Long live the Great Leader Chairman Mao.

We had all managed to master it quickly. Its basic moves were as follows: At "The respected Chairman Mao, you are the red sun in our hearts," we were supposed to raise our arms above our heads to show the utmost respect. When we came to "We have so many things to tell you," we first had to put our hands on our chests before reaching out our arms emotionally, as if we were really expressing the yearning of our hearts. At "We have so many songs to sing for you," we were supposed to hold our faces in our hands, eyes up, and fingers alternately retracting and extending as if radiating light. At "Millions of red hearts are poured out to you," we had to hold our thumbs and index fingers together in the shape of a heart on our chests. Then, as it came to "Millions of faces are smiling to the red sun," we'd hold our faces in our palms before twice reaching our arms up to the right. The dance ended when the song came to "Long live the Great Leader Chairman Mao," and we'd wave our *Little Red Books* or red silk kerchiefs.

This was my second time seeing Mao in person. I was thrilled, even though he was so far away that he was just a tiny dot up on the tower. As the song boomed from the loudspeakers, hundreds of thousands of people abandoned themselves to the dance.

Events at Tiananmen Square mirrored the nation's spirit in those years. A popular saying about the Dance of Loyalty was this: "It doesn't matter if you dance it well or not, but it does matter if you don't do it at all." Participation was proof of loyalty. Under this political pressure, everyone learned it. In some cities Red Guards stopped passersby at crossroads to test their skills. If they failed, they would be required to repeat the steps over and over until they mastered the dance. In the railway stations of Shijiazhuang and Shenyang, only those who could do the dance were allowed to board the trains.

One day, on my way back home, I saw a group of old women learning the dance. This didn't strike me as being particularly odd, for by then, many old people were eager to learn. One in particular stood out to me. A Han woman in her sixties, she was the most serious student in the bunch. She was sweating all over. Even while the other people were taking a break, she didn't stop practicing. Of all the ethnic groups in China, I later came to realize, singing and dancing came least easily to the Han people. It was quite likely that the old woman had never danced until that very day.

The Morning and Evening Rituals and the Dance of Loyalty were not the end of it. "Respect the Pioneering Spirit of the Masses" was yet another contrivance by which people exhibited their respect for Chairman Mao and his ideas.

Every day, China National Radio would broadcast a new saying from Chairman Mao late at night, and within a couple of hours, the saying had spread through all media channels across the country. To highlight the saying's importance, the newsreader from the radio station would announce it at "recording speed," which meant that not only the characters but also the punctuation marks were read aloud. Work units across the country stationed someone by the radio to write down everything on colored paper. The next day, people paraded through the streets with the new saying, an action called "a good news announcement." They played drums and gongs, setting off fireworks to generate a more festive atmosphere. The more people who gathered and the faster they did so, the more loyal the working unit and its people were thought to be.

Colleges across the country stopped functioning for ten years during the Cultural Revolution, but middle and primary school students were prodded back to the classroom in November 1967, and I was among the millions marching at school parades. Many a time we ventured all the way to Tiananmen Square on foot and then back. The next morning, our lessons were set aside as we all yawned and parroted our ways through the latest instructions from Chairman Mao. Independent thinking was neither expected nor tolerated; blind execution of orders issued from above sufficed. Everyone was like a grain of sand rolling within a dune.

One morning, a classmate named Lu and I went to buy some pens at a shop near our school. When we got there, shop assistants were performing their Morning Ritual. They stood in two lines, all in white frocks. With customers waiting patiently, they carried on with their ritual.

Inside the store, I noticed a change. On each counter was a notice: "To workers, peasants, and army men: every request made must be led by a quotation from Chairman Mao."

This was an era in which everything, or nearly everything, which people read or talked about had to start with a quotation, whether it was a newspaper story, a big-character poster, or chatting between friends. After a year of the Cultural Revolution, reciting Chairman Mao's quotations presented no difficulties to anyone. What they did in this department store was nothing unusual; it was just a way to show respect toward the Great Leader.

Even so, the dialogue between my classmate Lu and the shop assistant that day proved quite amusing.

"'Take good care of the lives of the people,'" Lu began. "I need a ballpoint pen."

The shop assistant, a girl in her twenties, replied, "'Serve the people wholeheartedly.' What kind of pen?"

"'We came from all over the country,'" Lu continued. "Please show us different varieties."

"'Combat liberalism,'" she retorted. "I won't allow that liberty. I'll just bring the one you want."

"'Our duty,'" Lu pleaded, "'is to hold ourselves responsible to the people.' I have no idea which pen is best for me. Please let me choose."

With a stern face, the girl said, "'On a question of two lines there is no room for compromise.' You're being fussy. As I said, no picking and choosing."

Lu was also displeased. "'We should support whatever the enemy opposes.' Why can't I make a selection?"

"'We should oppose whatever the enemy supports.' I repeat, no picking and choosing!"

"'Pay attention to the working method,'" Lu shot back. "You're not a good shop assistant!"

"'Power belongs to the Peasants' Association,'" said the girl. "Take it or leave it!"

Lu flared up. "'Down with local tyrants and evil gentry.' You really have an attitude problem."

"'Friendship or invasion?'" said the girl. "So you want to play hard ball?"

"'Everything reactionary is the same; if you don't hit it, it won't fall,'" Lu exclaimed, puffing in anger. "Am I supposed to be scared of you?"

Things had gotten out of control, so I pacified the situation by saying, "As Chairman Mao says, 'We need unity, not division,' so stop fighting and be reasonable. Anyway, we are revolutionary comrades."

But the shop assistant would not back down. "'Push the revolution to the end.' Who do you think you are?"

Lu proved dauntless. "'Those who do not offend should not be offended; those who offend shall be offended.' You're just a shop assistant behind your counter. Who do *you* think you are?"

"'When the enemy advances,'" I interrupted, "'we retreat, and when they retreat, we pursue.'" I turned to Lu. "Let's go and come back later."

At the doorway, Lu suddenly turned around. He shouted to the shop assistant, "'Farewell, Leighton Stuart!'" This was a reference to the United States ambassador to China, who been recalled when the Communists came into power in 1949.

The girl smiled primly, then changed her expression. "'All reactionaries are paper tigers,'" she shouted with her eyes bulging out. "Boo!"

SHATTERED MUSIC

SOMEONE WAS POUNDING ON OUR DOOR.

Fear prickled through me. It was an unforgivingly cold day in the spring of 1968. I locked eyes with Father. I was the only one of my siblings at home that day. My brother had been sent to Guangdong, our former home in the south of China, and my younger sister hadn't come back from school yet.

The knocks reverberated through the apartment. Just one kick would send the shabby wooden door flying off its hinges. With my heart in my throat, I rushed over to peek through the gauze opening we used as a peephole.

Five or six fierce-looking people were standing at the doorway. I knew the one standing closest to the door—his name was He and he was a hulking man of about six feet, three inches.

"Open up now or I'll kick the door down!" he barked.

The look on his face was enough to terrify me, but now

my heart started to kick against my chest. My hand shook as I gripped the doorknob, and I prepared myself for what was waiting for us on the other side.

✩✩✩

For the last few years, my father had been working as the chief of *Beijing Review's* Spanish-language division. The magazine was under the China Foreign Languages Publishing Bureau (CFLPB). Apart from *Beijing Review*, the bureau also oversaw other titles such as *People's China, People's Pictorial,* and *Reconstruct China.* In terms of infighting and conflict among different groups during the Cultural Revolution, this bureau probably saw more than any other in the country, a situation which coincided with the country's state of affairs in those days.

After Mao applauded Shanghai's January Revolution, angry words flashed and then devolved into violence. Once the rebels seized power, they set up revolutionary committees to replace the former government and Party committees. Something similar was now underway at *Beijing Review.* Chaos was spreading rapidly, even so far as to compromise the central government's own foreign policy. Extreme left-wingers harbored the illusion that China was at the center of a world revolution to rescue oppressed nations across the globe from what they saw as an abyss of suffering. China's foreign relations with the Soviet Union, the United States, the United Kingdom, and all of her neighboring countries suffered. Xenophobia gripped the homeland, as was demonstrated when the British Office in Beijing was set on fire. Many foreigners had come to China to work for publishing houses under the bureau. Now they quickly found themselves painted as political targets.

The situation was growing worse and worse. According to a report from the Xinhua News Agency, in March 1968, the Lanzhou Public Security Bureau had cracked an espionage case involving British spies. *People's Daily* published an article entitled "Fight Enemy Espionage: Consolidate Our Proletarian Dictatorship." Madame Mao issued this statement: "Many foreign workers in China seem friendly to China. . .but in fact they are agents of foreign secret services." This set off a nationwide campaign against foreigners. Some foreign nationals were kicked out of the country, while others were thrown into prison.

Beijing Review was actively involved in this campaign, routing out class enemies from the inside. My father had been subject to scrutiny before this—but this time, he was a key figure for investigation and public humiliation. It was under these conditions that disaster fell on our family.

✳✳✳

"Stay in your room," I whispered to my parents. Their faces were wracked with fear.

As soon as I pulled the door open, five or six people immediately pushed their way in. Apart from He, there was Li, whom I also knew, followed by three other people I didn't recognize. They tore through the apartment, quickly discovering Father and Mother in the back room.

"We've come to search for proof of espionage and rent collection!" Li shouted.

I knew we had no choice but to cooperate. Before he finished, the three young men had tied Father to a chair with a rope. Mother was instructed to stay in the corner, and not to do or say anything.

"You stay where you are," He said with a finger pointed at my nose, "or we'll kill you!"

I was furious, but I didn't dare show it. Over the previous two years of the Cultural Revolution, I'd grown accustomed to such scenes, and I was fully aware of the consequences if I didn't do as I was told. "These bastards come from a counterrevolutionary family," the intruders were muttering to each other.

By "bastards" he meant me. Because my father had been declared a "counterrevolutionary," my siblings and I were now underdogs to anyone, anywhere, and anytime.

The search was quickly underway. Father had brought three large armoires back from the U.S. when he finished his studies there. They were decorated with iron sheets and nails and each had a strong, old-fashioned bronze lock. To Cantonese people, armoires like these were greatly treasured. They were nothing less than works of art. My family's most important belongings were kept inside these three pieces of furniture.

"Open the doors," one of the men ordered, "or we'll smash them!"

Still tied to a chair, Father was unable to move.

I shot a look at Mother. She'd have to unlock the cupboards. For a moment the room was quiet as she produced the keys. Her hands were quivering as she worked the lock.

The rebels showed no restraint as they rifled through the contents of the armoires. They simply dumped everything on the floor.

First they tore through our photographs. My father had always loved photography. When he was a student in America, he'd bought a Leica camera with the money he'd made working various part-time jobs. As a young man he would never have expected that, years later, a group of rebels would take his photos as evidence that he'd served as a spy on behalf of American imperialism.

They pounced on three particular photographs. The first was of the Empire State Building in New York. The Empire State Building was, at the time, the tallest structure in the world. The next photograph was of Saint John's Cathedral in Manhattan. The rebels fingered it with obvious satisfaction. Coupled with the photograph of the Empire State Building, this picture would be enough to convict my father of a crime. He obviously "worshiped" the Empire State Building, the symbol of American Imperialism, and the photo of Saint John's Cathedral proved his collusion with counterrevolutionary Catholics. After all, wasn't the Vatican the most anti-revolutionary force in the world?

The third piece of "evidence" was my parents' wedding photo. In the black-and-white photograph, my father, a very handsome young man, is dressed in a Western-style suit with a bow tie; my mother is dressed in a white gown and she holds a bouquet of flowers in front of her. The wedding had taken place in 1948. My grandfather, who'd run an English school for Chinese students, was fairly wealthy at the time. The best photographer in Guangzhou had taken the wedding photo.

A few days before the rebels burst into our house, my father had sensed that something might happen. My parents' wedding photograph had until recently taken pride of place in their bedroom. Father locked it and some others inside the armoire for safekeeping.

But now that photograph became one of the rebels' trophies.

The wedding picture was framed in carved bronze. It was an elegant piece, although the years had taken their toll and it was scuffed and worn. One of the young men showed it to Li, their leader, who said simply, "Smash it!" The young man did what he was told, muttering "decadent bourgeois trash!"

The glass broke into tiny shards, scattering across the floor. One of the rebels bent down and shredded the photograph. But the strong frame remained intact. The young man grew angry—he threw the frame against the wall repeatedly until it was bent out of shape.

My mother was devastated, shouting tearfully in Cantonese, "It's ruined! My treasure!" Father was obviously infuriated. His eyes were bulging wildly. But he could do nothing with his arms bound to the chair. Mother tried to pick up the photo, but then one of the men yanked her back by the hair and pushed her down on the bed.

"Please—" I said, trying to reason with them. The rebel named He approached me from behind and kicked my shin. I whipped around. "Behave yourself," He warned. "Don't you know the crime your father has committed?" I didn't reply. "You should be thankful," he added, "that we're letting your father stay home instead of locking him up in prison!" He emphasized his point with another kick. Another young man in an army uniform sidled up to He and added, "Tie him up if he resists."

I was furious, but I couldn't show it. As a reporter for the campus newspaper for the past two years, I had witnessed too many cases like this. I was fully aware of how brutal the rebels could be, of the pain they were capable of inflicting on their victims. I was still just a teenager and no match for these men. I kept my silence.

Later my sister would tell me the fate of the photographs the rebels had found in our home. They were put on public display in an exhibition held in the CFLPB as a demonstration of the success of searching homes to collect evidence of crimes. The photos were taken as indisputable proof of my father's treachery.

The rebels continued the search in high spirits. Before long, they made another discovery: an English typewriter in a black aluminum case with a lock at the bottom. They tried to open the lock but failed. At the end of their wits, they forced it open with a hammer. When they saw the keyboard spokes inside, they believed that they had found a small transmitter used by spies.

Next they came across a small valve radio receiver made in Shanghai. The radio suffered the same fate as the typewriter. The speaker was cut off with a pair of scissors.

My heart sank. That radio had always been special to me. I'd been listening to it when I first heard the news that

Chinese table tennis player Rong Guotuan had won the championship in the Twenty-Sixth World Table Tennis Tournament, the first world table tennis champion in Chinese history. Not much later, Rong Guotuan, who was by then living in exile, was tortured and eventually committed suicide.

The search continued. Next up was our glass book cabinet, which had also been imported from the United States. It was crammed with Father's treasured volumes of classic literature. He'd come to love Walt Whitman's poetry when he was in the U.S.; after he'd returned to China, he published a Chinese translation of *The Life of Walt Whitman*. When I was very young, he told me to read *Leaves of Grass* and to ask him to explain anything that puzzled me. *Gone with the Wind* was another of his favorites. A book about life on a farm in the southern part of the U.S., he'd eventually read it many times before he died. Another favorite was Tolstoy's *War and Peace*.

These books, together with others inside the cabinet such as *The Complete Works of William Shakespeare*, were destroyed—torn up, stamped on, and dumped in the toilet. Even classical Chinese works such as *The Dynamic Histories from Remote Antiquity to the Ming Dynasty* and different editions of Tang and Song dynasty poems were dubbed "poisonous herbs from feudalism, capitalism, and revisionism" and were now ravaged. *Only The Dream of Red Mansions* survived. Chairman Mao liked it, so it was spared.

Next the rebels noticed our gramophone and records. Both Father and Mother loved music. The 33-rpm gramophone was accompanied by numerous albums, all of them by classical composers: Beethoven, Johann Straus (both senior and junior), Chopin, and Mozart. Among this group, Mozart was Father's favorite. He had told me stories about Mozart when I was a young boy. "A great musician who died young," Father called him, "and a man who bequeathed to humanity many marvelous pieces of music." Categorized as "absolute music," these works were now banned.

The rebels took away the gramophone and some of the records. The rest were smashed right then and there. Then, after a two-hour-long search-and-destroy mission, they gathered up their "evidence" and left.

✷✷✷

As soon as we were alone, I untied Father from the chair. By then, Mother had fainted from all the crying.

We sat together in stunned silence, staring at the ruin the rebels had wrought.

The floor was covered with damaged books, records, and torn clothing. The rebels had taken away Father's Western-style suits and Mother's high-heeled shoes and dresses. These were "proof" of my parents' inclination toward a bourgeoisie lifestyle.

After some minutes my sister Si Yan returned home, took one look at the state of the house, and burst into tears.

Father was fairly calm now. As a veteran of China's War of Resistance against the Japanese, he had received a medal from the Chinese government on the 60th anniversary of the day of victory. His composure likely stemmed from his service in the army. He picked up a damaged record. It was *The Blue Danube*, warped and clearly no longer playable. Still, he dusted it carefully before putting it into the record jacket. Without speaking a word, he did the same with all the other albums scattered on the floor.

In 2005, when he was in his eighties, he'd take Mother to visit the hometowns of both Tolstoy and Shakespeare. That year he also asked me to accompany them to a concert at the Wiener Musikverein, a concert hall in Vienna. Much to his delight, he was able to visit Mozart's former residence in Salzburg as well.

"This has been the greatest satisfaction in my life," he told me afterwards.

I nodded, then said, "Do you still remember the time they came and searched our home?" My tone was light, almost jovial.

He fell silent for a while before he replied. "Too painful to look back."

There was at least one blessing on that day. Father was not a Christian, but on the wall of my family home in Guangzhou he'd hung a plaster figurine of Jesus Christ, which he had brought back with him from New York City. When we moved to Beijing, the figurine came with us. Months before the search, he'd had a premonition of the trouble to come. He wrapped the figurine with old newspapers and smashed it. He then threw the pieces away. The rebels would have punished us even more brutally if they'd found that small statue, no question. It was an irreverent act, I'd later think, but one that Jesus himself would likely have forgiven.

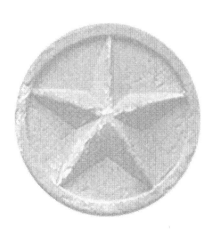

DEFIANCE

ONE SUNDAY NOT LONG AFTER THE REBELS RAIDED OUR apartment, Father was instructed to report to the authorities for further questioning.

With my sixth uncle and fifth aunt living in the U.S. at the time, Father was believed to have "suspicious overseas relations." The questions they shot at Father included: "When did you go there and where did you stay?" "How do you get in touch with your younger brother in the U.S.?" "What is he doing there?" "Where did you stay in the U.S.?" "How have you continued to work for the U.S. government since returning to China?"

During his interrogation, Father was told to keep his head low while answering questions. One look directly in the interrogators' eyes and he would be slapped in the face. But my father was an obstinate character—how could he accept charges for something he had never done? The slapping, punching, and kicking continued to rain down on his slender frame. The interrogators even used clubs wrapped in rubber. Each time Father refused to speak, a new round of beatings would begin. Eventually he began crawling on the floor from one corner to another, trying to escape.

Even so, Father continued to deny the charges. He simply shouted at the top of his voice, asking the interrogators to stop. This was like pouring fuel on the fire, for more torture followed. One punch to Father's forehead totally knocked him out. They had to use cold water to bring him back to consciousness, and then they began beating him again.

✯✯✯

The sad memory of taking my father to the hospital after that interrogation would never leave me. It had been a snowy day. Father had been gone for hours and the sky was now dark. Looking out of the window from the second floor of our apartment, I suddenly saw two rebels hauling him back home. I tore out of the apartment and down to the courtyard. By the time I reached him he'd fallen on the ground, and I had to summon all my strength to pull him back to his feet and march him upstairs.

The moment I got him inside, he collapsed. He had no strength left to say anything. After we fixed him up in bed, we saw wounds on his face and body. He wanted to use the toilet, but had no strength left to stand up. I took him a bedpan. Later, when I came to take it away, I saw blood.

I felt so hopeless. Father had always been so strong, but now he was moaning in pain. Obviously he had a bone fracture or some internal bleeding. We couldn't get an ambulance or a doctor to come examine him at home. All I could do was jump onto my bike and ride to the nearest pharmacy to buy iodine, gauze, and simple medicines for the cuts. With them, we dressed his wounds.

What happened the next day was even worse. We paid a fortune to take a taxi to the hospital. In those days, the average monthly salary per person was only about thirty *yuan*, but that trip cost us about a week's wages. I didn't mind the cost, but it soon proved to be a waste.

"What happened to him?" asked a middle-aged male doctor.

"Just some wounds," I said, trying to sound casual.

Father was moaning in pain. Did he have a kidney hemorrhage or a bone fracture? The doctor opened his jacket to take a look.

He was clearly stupefied. "These wounds are from a beating," he said. "The hospital is unable to take care of him. Only counterrevolutionaries and bad people of other sorts are beaten up like this." There was nothing he could do, he emphasized.

Was this a joke? I couldn't believe my ears. A medical doctor standing before a man in severe pain and refusing to help him?

I dropped to my knees. "Please," I begged, "please help my father. He may die if he has internal bleeding!"

He hesitated just for a moment, then said, "I wish I could, but if I did, I would get in trouble. The rebels will come to give me trouble. These things have happened before. That's why the hospital has made a rule and there are no exceptions."

I telephoned another hospital. They hung up on me even before I finished speaking. The message was clear: No hospital would treat a man with my father's type of injuries.

I was shocked, and also grief-stricken. How could the world have become this callous, this cold? But this was no time to lament or to blame anyone. As the only able man left in the family, I couldn't lose my head. A classmate of mine, I remembered, had a father who practiced medicine. I quickly phoned him for help. My classmate's father told me that the urinal bleeding came from a wounded kidney and that antibiotics were needed. If my father had pain in his back, he might have had a bone fracture somewhere. Antibiotics first, he suggested, then bed rest.

In despair, I helped Father out of that hospital. We had no more money for a taxi. Bus 32 was the only option. Nobody on board yielded a seat to Father. Nobody was willing even to lift a finger and help. Father simply collapsed in the aisle.

But my prayers to heaven were answered. The antibiotic I obtained at my classmate's father's suggestion was penicillin. It worked wonderfully. I also applied medical paste to Father's open wounds and rubbed his swollen spots with turpentine.

Several days later, when Father said he had regained his appetite, I rushed to the nearest restaurant on my bike to buy stewed bean curd with minced pork in pepper sauce. Tears of joy filled my eyes as he ate.

✻✻✻

When he recovered, Father told us what had happened before the interrogation. He felt terribly aggrieved that the young man named Li, his subordinate, had been so cruel to him. Father had been very nice to this young man. I knew him, too. Once, when Father caught a cold and had to stay home to rest, Li had cooked porridge for him. He was a newcomer, having served in the army before coming to the newspaper. Before leaving he said to me in a very gentle voice, "Take good care of your father. Use a little salt when you make porridge; it will cook easily and taste better." How could such a man torture my father?

There were two main charges against Father: first, that he was working as a spy for the U.S. government, and second, that he was exploiting people in Guangzhou, where he collected rents. The evidence the rebels produced to support these charges were none other than the photos of the Empire State Building and Saint John's Cathedral that they had taken away during the raid.

The charge about collecting rent circled back to my grandfather. My grandfather came from a very poor family that had sold pickled fish for a living. But he was a hard-working student. Because of his excellent record, he'd been recommended for study in Japan by the famous scholar Liang Qichao. After returning to China, he published the first English grammar book for Chinese students. Many universities still used it in their curricula. The government seized his properties in Guangzhou and Hong Kong after the founding of New China, but they left some for his descendants to use. Over time my father had rented them out to a few people who needed places to live. The rent my parents collected was now regarded as exploitation, a "very serious crime" according to then-current political standards.

There was no way around it: my father was guilty of this charge.

But the second charge—that Father was a U.S. spy—struck me as absurd. As a student in America, he'd paid his tuition partially by working part-time in restaurants. Back in Hong Kong, when he was asked—as the eldest son in the family—to inherit the business my grandfather had started, Father refused. He believed his country needed him, and he insisted on returning to Mainland China. Nothing could change the will of a young man like my father, and so my tearful grandfather saw him off at the port of Luohu, where barbed wire separated the Communist mainland from British Hong Kong. The old man didn't know that this meeting with his son would be his last.

Father couldn't possibly be a spy. It just didn't square with anything I knew about him, not even slightly.

⋆⋆⋆

Next came this news: a struggle session had been scheduled at our home. I was already terrified that the rebels would return to search our home again, but now I became even more nervous. I simply had to protect my parents, I kept saying to myself.

The rebels placed a great deal of importance on this event. Wang, the leader of the rebels targeting Father, had called me in three separate times to discuss the speeches my family and I were expected to make during the struggle session. "You have to take a clear-cut stand," she said. "You can't blur the line between right and wrong. You must expose the crimes your father has committed."

The first speech I wrote didn't pass muster. Neither did the second. Infuriated, Wang threatened to schedule even more struggle sessions at our home unless we "stopped being smart."

In those moments I thought she was the ugliest, filthiest, and meanest woman I had ever met. I couldn't even stand to look at her, but I kept reminding myself that for my parents' sake I had to endure everything. *Only two things are important*, I said to myself. *One, persuade Father to cooperate, and two, make a speech good enough to placate the rebels.*

In order to reach a consensus, we held a family meeting. I took the role of chairing it. "In a couple of days," I began, "the rebels will be here. This is a crisis for the whole family, and we have to act as one to weather the storm."

Father hadn't yet recovered from the latest series of beatings and interrogations. All he could do was lie in bed and nod his head in agreement. Mother, meanwhile, was in tears. She said nothing.

Later, I spoke to Father while applying an ointment to his back. The beatings had left bloody welts on his skin, and he flinched each time I touched him.

"I have learned a phrase that I think is useful in these times," I began. "It is, 'A wise man never swims against the tide.' Now the tide is against us and we have to face this."

Working the ointment gently into his wounds, I told him he should on no account accept the charge of being a U.S. spy. That would land him in jail, there was no doubt about it. The charge of leading a bourgeois lifestyle was something that we could accept, particularly since the rebels now had the photos and records as proof. We should play a kind of ideological sleight of hand, I said. Because they also had evidence of the rent collection in Guangzhou, we could accept that charge as well. That wasn't enough to put us in jail. Why not make them happy for the time being?

"The Party's been trying to do away with capitalists and landlords," I added. "Since they never worked for what they earned, isn't it exploitation to collect rent from the people? That was a sin, wasn't it?"

At this, Father was silent. Then he said that he too regretted what had happened. He had dealt with the properties he'd inherited from Grandfather without thinking things through. He'd thought that his brothers and sisters could share the rent and that this was, to him, the duty of the eldest son in the family.

"Fine," he said at last, "I'll do as you say."

✯✯✯

With this conversation behind me, I now turned my attention to writing everyone's speeches for the struggle session. The one my sister was to make was fairly easy to compose; nobody would take a 13-year-old girl at her word. By simply copying phrases from the newspaper and big-character posters, it was done.

But the speech I was to make did matter—a lot. I needed to have Chairman Mao's quotations at the ready, and the more the better. I also had to show an adequate awareness of the "crimes" Father had committed.

I poured all my energy into my speech. I concentrated on Father's purported "worship" of the "decadent American

lifestyle." For this I drew my support from none other than
Lenin, who'd said that imperialism was dying, this being the
final stage of decadent capitalism. I was very pleased with
this quotation. My father thought he had seen the Empire
State Building, I said, but no, he hadn't actually seen it. The
building was crumbling, ready to collapse at any time. It was
a symbol of decadence. There was no hope, no future to it.

On the subject of rent collection, I quoted Chairman Mao.
I knew the rebels would like this. Exploitation, I said, was
to withhold surplus value. I was very proud of the phrase
"surplus value" as it was fashionable at the time. Although
the property had come from my grandfather, I added, and
was private property, Father had never contributed his labor,
so how could he collect money from the people who rented
it? What was this if not exploitation? Exploitation, taking
surplus value from other people, should never be tolerated.
It had to be punished.

Although I wasn't an especially skilled writer, my train of
thought was clear, and I bolstered my ideas with important-
sounding words from the big-character posters I'd
encountered over the previous two years. I kept silent on the
most serious charges while admitting minor ones, a tactic
people in such situations often used at the time.

Equally important was the speech Mother was to make.
I was very worried as I started laying it out. How could I
make it sound like it was written by my mother? And how
could I explain actions? Over the years she'd indeed gone
to Guangzhou to collect rent on the family's properties.
After she was seriously reprimanded, she was often seen
weeping at home.

"She's in poor health," I'd told Wang. "Can I make it short

for her? Besides," I added, "it was always my father who sent her to collect rent."

Wang said nothing, and I took it as a sign of approval. I decided to write a piece in my mother's voice, angrily accusing Father of forcing her to collect rent from tenants.

I'd already finished the speech for my younger sister. I had hoped Mother would be able to practice her speech, but the look on her face convinced me it was a bad decision. So I read it for her. My sister Si Yan blinked her eyes. She looked at Father and then Mother. After I read my speech, none of the family spoke. My sister was obviously angry.

"You said that Father was bad," she accused me, "and I don't like it."

"Unless we do this," I said, trying to pacify her, "we're going to be in for a much harder time. Father's already agreed. It's a trick to win the trust of our enemies."

All the speeches I wrote passed the rebels' scrutiny. I'm still surprised when I look back on it today. That experience made me, at that point not yet sixteen years old, much stronger. I behaved like a man. My education, however wanting in certain respects, had served me well. The past two years of the Cultural Revolution had been a classroom in which I learned what real life was, what beauty and ugliness, brutality and loyalty, were. Now it was time to prove just how well I had learned those lessons.

Photo of the author's family taken at the end of 1967, a few months before the family struggle session. Seated in front are the parents. Standing, from left to right: Si Yan, the author's younger sister, the author, and his elder brother Xu Yang.

THE STRUGGLE SESSION

DOWN WITH COUNTERREVOLUTIONARY ZHAO!" SOMEONE shouted, and then "Down with landowner Qin!"

The struggle session had begun.

"Now," said Wang in a booming voice, "Reactionary Zhao and Landowner Qin, come and plead guilty before Chairman Mao's picture."

Father and Mother were forced to walk gingerly toward the photograph. They bent down and lowered their heads toward the ground.

Raising the *Little Red Book* to her chest, Wang barked, "Revolutionary comrades, stand up and say, 'Long live Chairman Mao—'"

This was standard procedure, a must at every denunciation. Everyone around us echoed her.

"Good health to Vice-Chairman Lin Biao," she continued. Terrified, we followed suit.

"Let us sing 'The East Is Red,' shouted Wang. This old

folk song had been rearranged to honor Mao and the Communist Party of China. It went like this:

> The East is red, the sun rises.
> China has brought forth one Mao.
>
> He amasses fortune for the people, Hurrah,
> He is the people's liberating star.
>
> Chairman Mao loves the people,
> He is our guide,
>
> To build a new China, Hurrah,
> He leads us forward!
>
> The Communist Party is like the sun,
> Wherever it shines, there is light.
>
> Wherever there is a Communist Party,
> Hurrah, there the people are free and happy!

My parents were forbidden to sing, but my younger sister and I were permitted to join the chorus. Loyalty to Chairman Mao and the Communist Party had been bred into our blood. We'd recited this song with sincerity countless times, but on this particular day, political loyalty and family devotion stood in stark opposition. Where we'd once felt pride we now felt something else: confusion and rage.

"Now, keep your heads lows and turn around!" yelled Wang. "It's time to receive denouncement from the revolutionary people!"

My heart sank to see my father's beaten and bloody face. My mother was still shaking and it seemed like she might pass out.

It was time now to receive the highest instructions from Chairman Mao. With the treasured Little Red Book clasped to her chest, Wang recited a couple of Chairman Mao's quotations from memory. I'd never forget the two quotations she recited on that day: "Never forget class struggle!" and "Everything reactionary is the same. If you don't hit it, it won't fall. This is also like sweeping the floor. As a rule, where the broom doesn't reach, the dust will not vanish of its own accord."

Now the denunciation officially began. It was Wang who announced my father's crimes. There were two separate charges: first, my father was working as a spy for the U.S. government, second, my parents were exploiting people by collecting rent. The evidence the rebels produced to support these charges were two photos they'd taken when ransacking our apartment just days before of the Empire State Building and Saint John's Cathedral in New York.

This, I thought, was laughable, but were my parents guilty of the other crime, collecting rent? I understood that this charge had to do with my grandfather's properties, but as soon as Father's crimes were announced, the angry shouts started up and terror interrupted my thoughts.

Some of those shouting were rebels, while others were our neighbors. One of them was a pregnant woman in her thirties with a small child in her arms. She had come for the spectacle. My mother was told later that every family had been instructed by the neighborhood committee to send one person to the meeting. That pregnant woman was the only one available in her family.

Father's face reddened with anger, and Mother's hands shook. Holding my sister's hand, I tried to comfort her. Suddenly, I noticed Father's face change. I'd been monitoring his mental state for weeks, but I realized now that I'd missed something. Chinese culture held that "no man's crime involves his wife and children," but on that day, at that particular meeting, his wife and children were being humiliated for his "crimes." How could a man with a strong sense of self-respect take this, having his family publicly humiliated along with him? But he had to endure it. The fate of his family members was now in his hands.

I knew Father was innocent. He couldn't be a spy working for anyone. Amid the thunderous slogans, I suddenly remembered a song that Father had taught me when I was a little boy. "Graduation," it was called, and it was meant to encourage young people to join the resistance war against the Japanese in northern Guangdong. Both its tune and lyrics were deeply inspiring:

Rise, school mates, take responsibility for our country!
The rise and fall of the nation is in our hands!

Listen to the miserable cries of the nation.
We have lost our territory day by day.

To rise and fight, or to stay low and surrender—that is the question!
As masters of the country, we prefer to die on the battleground.

We refuse to be enslaved,
Even it means being safe and sound.

Today, we are tree branches;
Tomorrow, we will be the pillars of the nation.

Today, we are singing together;
Tomorrow, we will join the salvation work to
make a difference.

We are pure waves that continue to rise.
Fellow schoolmates, lend your hands to build a
strong nation.

How could someone who loved a song like this be a traitor? "Trust me," my father had once told me, "I have never done anything against this country."

Yes, I trusted him, but it wasn't enough to help him now.

"And now!" shouted Wang after the slogans had been shouted. "Qin is about to expose the crimes her reactionary husband has committed."

Mother didn't respond. She was shuddering terribly. *Come on, Mother*, I said to myself, *look this way, please!* I wanted to give her a look of encouragement, but her eyes were fixed on Father. To her, nothing and no one else existed. "Quickly," someone prompted from the side. "Stop playing the fool!"

At this, she hastily produced two sheets of paper from her pocket and began to read quickly. It was obvious she wanted to finish the task as soon as possible.

Nothing prepared me for the moment when the rebels began beating Mother.

She'd started off fairly well, but before long, she began to sob and she was unable to continue. When someone shouted at her to continue, Mother shuddered even more. "Landowner!" came the booming voice. "Who do you think you are?"

I looked around the room. I saw the eyes around us—some cold, others faintly sympathetic. No one dared speak in her defense.

Of all the rebels, it was He who was the most degenerate. Even when my father had bowed his head to the lowest point, he still wasn't happy. He pushed father's head even lower. Sitting in a chair next to me, he crossed one leg over the other in a most arrogant posture. His filthy shoes nearly touched my nose. For a second, it felt like a nightmare, an illusion. *Please,* I prayed, *let this be over quickly.*

Suddenly, Mother burst out hysterically, "No, no more of this!"

I was jolted back to reality. Father quickly turned to hold Mother in his arms. My sister rushed up to help. It seemed that Mother was at the edge of a nervous breakdown. She was wailing uncontrollably.

For a moment, the rebels seemed at a loss. *Be calm,* I kept reminding myself. I turned to Wang. "My mother is having a mental breakdown," I said, "and she really can't continue. Let me do it for her." After consulting with someone, Wang told me to read my speech first. Mother's speech, she said, would have to wait until she regained her composure.

I felt like shouting at the heavens. But my good sense told me to control my anger. The rebels told my father to stand still, while I helped Mother sit in a chair. I told my sister to comfort her by holding her hand.

After it quieted down, I began. *I must make the rebels happy*, I kept telling myself, *otherwise, everything we worked for will be for nothing!* I bottled my anger and fear. My voice was firm and determined as I spoke, not a note less earnest than any revolutionary could be.

The rebels gave me a pass.

Next came my younger sister. While she read her speech, I took my mother's hand in mine.

"Your turn," one of the rebels demanded, training his eyes on Mother. "Finish your denunciation now."

I looked at Wang. My eyes were begging her to spare my mother. She was, however, more revolutionary than human. "Qin," I heard her cold voice address Mother, "go and finish your speech." Of all the words she'd said, these were probably the coldest and most ruthless I'd ever heard. Yet I dared not show my anger. I just hoped that this meeting would be over soon. "Please go and finish the reading," I whispered into Mother's ear, "and they will leave."

Mother seemed to pull herself together. She stood up to continue, but her whole body shook with emotion. The rebel He was angry. He kicked Mother and shouted, "Stand up properly!"

The kick sent her crashing to the floor. This happened so suddenly that the paper she was holding fell from her hands. She started screaming once again.

Father went down on his knees trying to help her back to her feet. His eyes were burning with anger. "You son of a bitch!" he shouted. "You're an animal!"

I couldn't believe my ears when I heard these words coming from his mouth.

Everyone was taken aback. It was quiet for a moment as we all waited to see how He would respond.

His whole face turned red as he turned to the crowd. "Look, this counterrevolutionary is challenging us!"

He received no response. Maybe the people around us did have some human decency left in them after all.

He sprang to his feet, finger pointing at my father's face as he began his angry accusation. "No humanity to class enemies! Comrade Lei Feng once said that we should be warm to comrades, but cold to enemies as an autumn wind sweeps fallen leaves. Lei Feng is an example Mao set for us. Do you dare deny this?"

The muscles in Father's face were quivering. After a long painful shriek, he collapsed onto the floor.

This clearly pleased Rebel He. "Never forget class struggle," he led the crowd in shouting. "Down with counterrevolutionary Zhao!"

I rushed forward, trying to help Father back to his feet. He was unable to stand because his wounds had not yet healed. He fell again. This was more than I could endure.

I pointed at Rebel He. "According to Chairman Mao," I shouted, "we should be having a verbal struggle, not resorting to violence. Why did you beat my father with a rubber stick in your basement until he was pissing blood? Are these really Chairman Mao's teachings? You're against the Great Leader. Worse, you're sabotaging the Cultural Revolution!"

My sister was in tears. "You are a bad person!" she shouted. "You beat people up!"

He couldn't reply. The whole situation was coming apart. Fury overwhelmed me. I wished I could pick up a sharp knife from the kitchen to stab Rebel He. But no, I wouldn't have done that. Even at that point, I still wasn't quite carried away with rage. After all, I had to keep my parents safe. I forced myself to stay silent. After I'd helped Father onto the bed and Mother to a chair, I walked up to Rebel Wang. My sister stood beside me, her hand in mine. I just looked at her without saying anything.

"What do you want?" she asked.

"With everyone present, I have a favor to ask."

"Go ahead. Ask it."

"Everybody can see the state both my father and mother are in now. Let me and my younger sister receive your denunciation so that we can take them to the hospital." I closed my eyes. Tears streamed down my face. I didn't lift a hand to dry them. I didn't want to make a sound. I wanted them to flow out at will until they were no more.

There was a short silence, then the commotion resumed. I didn't care anymore what the rebels would do to me. As I stood there all I could see on the balcony was a rope made with strips of old clothing. It had been put there in case of an emergency. "If the rebels come," Father had said, "we can use it to escape." Later, my younger sister told me that the first time she'd seen it, she'd let out an anguished cry because she thought that Father would use it to commit suicide. If anyone saw the rope and asked about it, Father said to my younger sister, she should simply say we used it for our laundry.

By the time I regained my senses, the struggle session was

over. The rebels were gone, leaving only my family behind. I saw people disappearing outside. Their scurrying figures meant nothing to me. I pulled myself together. The bad luck wasn't over, I warned myself, and misfortune might catch up with us yet again. The rebels, my sister told me, hadn't been satisfied with the struggle session. They'd said they would come back for another one pretty soon.

They never did. Events like those happening inside the CFLPB, as well as inside *Beijing Review* magazine, had come to the attention of the central government. Premier Zhou Enlai personally intervened. Several months later, my parents and sister were sent to Henan for "re-education" in the countryside, while I was forced to leave Beijing to do farm work in northern Shaanxi.

The Cultural Revolution continued, but we never experienced another struggle session. One reason was this: the five members of my family would soon be scattered in different places, far away and no longer able to bear witness to one another's pain.

As part of his re-education, the author was sent to live in the countryside. Here he poses with his friend and fellow cave dweller.

The author during harvest time. Life on the Loess Plateau proved a ceaseless challenge.

The author revisited the old cave residence on the Loess Plateau in 2006. He had a narrow escape when the cave collapsed in autumn of 1970.

EXILE ON THE
LOESS PLATEAU

THE BUS SPED WESTWARD OUT OF BEIJING, PLOWING THROUGH the snowy and pitch-dark streets. It was February 2, 1969, and I'd just graduated from the Beijing School of Foreign Languages. This had nothing to do with passing any courses; in fact, I hadn't even completed the first year's curriculum.

The school had no choice but to graduate me. The first three years of the Cultural Revolution—by far the most turbulent of the revolution—were over. Society was stabilizing, and schools were preparing to enroll new students. My school simply needed to make room for the incoming classes.

All across the country, a strange phenomenon was taking place: all six grades, from middle school to high school, were graduating at the same time. But where would all these new graduates find jobs? The answer came in the form of a new directive from Chairman Mao: "It is absolutely necessary for educated young people to be re-educated by poor and middle-class peasants in the countryside."

As one of those "educated" young people, I was ordered to leave Beijing for the Loess Plateau, where I was to receive a "re-education" from the peasantry.

The weather was foul on the day I left. At about six in the morning, I set out from home with a large bag strapped to my back. Father carried my suitcase, while Mother and my younger sister trailed behind. None of us spoke. As soon as we opened the door, a strong wind sent snowflakes dancing into the apartment.

"I'll be fine on my own," I reassured Mother.

My sister could no longer hold her emotions back, suddenly collapsing into Mother's arms and sobbing, "No, I want to go, I want to see my brother off!"

At this, Mother shook her head, but there were tears in her eyes, too. In the end, the whole family braved fierce winds and snow to see me off at the station.

It was still quite dark outside when we headed out. The streetlights cast amber beams across the snow. My whole family was silent, exposed to the merciless whiplash of the cold wind and falling snow. This was actually the second separation my family had been through; the first had been my brother's forced departure for Guangdong Province.

By the light of the streetlamp, I saw a look of hopelessness in Father's eyes. Still a target at work, he'd had to make repeated entreaties before obtaining permission from the rebels to accompany me that day. He'd always been exceptionally strong, the pillar of our family, but after losing my elder brother to the countryside in Guangdong and now

snow. Soaked through, the soil looked darker than its usual yellow, standing out in strong contrast like a black-and-white expanse.

All around me, snowflakes continued to fall soundlessly. A strange noise drifted up from the nearby ravines, probably carried by the wind. I stood motionless for a while, then I started to stamp my feet and rub my hands against my frozen cheeks. *Is this a dream?* I asked myself.

No, it wasn't a dream, I realized, coming to my senses. There was no going back to Beijing and to my family. This forbidding, empty place was now my home.

I turned around and stepped back into the cave. Dwellings like these were probably the earliest homes of our distant ancestors. This cave had actually been formed by cutting into the vertical face of a mountain slope, tunneling an arch from the front, and finishing it off with a window and a door. It was old and from the look of it hadn't been used in quite a while. On the right side was an empty sheepfold, while on the left was a much smaller cave with a short wall of broken bricks in the front. A "toilet," I realized with a shudder.

I would share this space with another "educated youth" from Beijing by the name of Huang Meng, one of thirty of us to be sent to the countryside. That first morning he was still sound asleep in the earthen bed. I didn't want to wake him, so I continued to look around quietly. About 200-odd square feet in size, the cave's walls and ceiling were darkened with soot. The bed and the earthen stove with an iron pot on top were the only pieces of furniture. The wooden window was in a shabby condition; covered with a tattered paper, it was singing in the wind, a chilly song of welcome or pity. Even the door seemed to complain about its lot: each time it was opened or closed, it gave a moaning sound.

★★★

The village, Zhengzhuang, was in Yanchang County, Yanan. It sat in the depths of the Loess Plateau. The local peasants, I soon discovered, were not exactly happy to see us. I found out why later on: This village had been grouped together with four smaller ones—about 200 households in total— that were scattered over four hills. Due to the trend of "collectivization," the smaller villages had been used for four sub-production teams—but before long, they were grouped together to become the Zhengzhuang Production Brigade, a team of eight-hundred members. Each team was paid according to the book of the new brigade, which had nothing to do with their original one.

The land here was barren, and due to serious water and soil erosion, the harvest was always poor. The only way to feed the people was by extensive cultivation. Every year, after handing in the agricultural taxes paid in grain, each person had only about a hundred kilos of food left. Our arrival meant there were thirty more mouths to feed, and without an increase in field acreage, the local peasants had no reason to be happy we were there.

Zhengzhuang was not the only village facing a dire food shortage. By one estimate, Sichuan Province, which had a population of one-hundred million, had less than one-sixth an acre per head. In the provinces, the food shortage was exacerbated by the sudden appearance of the large numbers of people cast out of Beijing—which is to say, people like me.

We didn't want to take food away from anybody, but we had to survive, and we had to appear on their books. We'd have to work longer hours than the villagers if we wanted to have enough food. The points were an index to show the value of our daily labor: Local male peasants earned ten points a day, while those of us from the outside earned only seven or eight points (males) or six points (females). The amount of food you were given from the autumn harvest depended on the number of points you earned.

My first job was to help build a new reservoir. In high spirits, my cohorts and I were all eager to prove our sense of collectivism and heroism. The task was to create two walls using the rocks in a gully before ramming the soil very solidly in between them. The ramming tool was no more than a block of stones, rounded in shape and flat at the bottom. Four of us pulled very strong ropes that were tied to it. As long as we timed it right, our combined strength would throw it up into the air so that it would fall downwards, ramming the soil with its weight.

The job demanded good coordination. You had to exert your utmost strength, while at the same time singing the rammers' working chant. In a way, it was like a song and dance performance. A single run-through of this method was enough to make anyone sweat all over.

After we finished the first day, my hands were covered with many bleeding blisters. But I was happy, very happy. I thought I'd proven myself. When the winter was over and the new dam was up, I felt a strong sense of accomplishment, though it was tempered with a bitter memory: a local peasant had been killed while blasting a rocky mount. It was a sobering lesson that our safety wasn't guaranteed in this place.

In the spring, we plowed the fields for sowing. The northern Shaanxi dialect fascinated me. Many of its phrases were philosophical in nature, bringing out the truth behind what was spoken. "To labor" in the Shaanxi dialect, for instance, was "to toil and suffer." "Falling sick" was to suffer. Spring was a busy season, and there was no time to lose. Every morning at five o'clock, while the sky was still dark, someone called out from the foot of the hill, "Time to toil and suffer!" That "folk song" was our morning wake-up call.

One job was by far the most difficult. Local fields were barren, so human excrement had become a precious resource, and not a single drop of it was to be spilled along the way. Following the production brigade's method, the first step was to extract the dung from appointed family "toilets"—earthen pits—and then mix the dung with fine soil before carrying the mixture to designated fields. I didn't really know how hard life was in this village until I was charged with this task. I would take a small path carrying the mixture down to a gully below, where there was a river and flatland. Walking was fairly easy, but just a couple of kilometers down there was a slope. My job each day was to carry five loads' worth of human waste. For this I earned a meager seven points.

Once, when I was exhausted, I tripped and took a bad

fall. The dung barrels broke loose from my pole and rolled into the distance. I hurriedly picked myself up, timidly looking around to see if anybody had noticed. Fortunately, nobody had witnessed the accident, and the barrels were intact. Carefully, I cupped the spilled excrement back into the barrels and beat a hasty retreat.

Sowing the fields was much easier. Oxen were brought in to help where it was steep, and where it wasn't, a hoe was used. A man would dig a small pit in front, followed by a woman who placed seeds carefully into it. I followed behind them both, spreading excrement on the fields to finish the procedure.

Digging ditches counted as both technical and manual labor, fetching a full ten points a day. The first time I took on the number-three job to the rear, I made a terrible show of myself. On that day, the old man—my neighbor—was in front digging the pits; his daughter, with a willow basket full of corn seeds hanging from her neck, was the second; while I, the third, finished up with the manure. Into every pit the old man made, his daughter dropped a couple of seeds. To the best of my understanding, my job was to spread the manure thickly onto each pit before I stamped the soil solid on top of it, but the daughter coughed to get her father's attention.

The old man turned around. "My dear city boy," he said, "this is not the way to do this job." He picked up a small handful of excrement from my bag, bending down to place it carefully on top of the seeds before moving the soil back in the same careful manner. "Good harvest or not," he said to me, "the manure decides. Make every lump count!"

Shamefaced, I nodded in agreement.

That was the moment I fully understood the hard work behind every grain of crop that was harvested. A famous Tang Dynasty poem came to mind:

> At noon when the sunshine is strongest,
> The farmer is weeding in his field with a hoe,
> His sweat drips onto the soil,
> Each grain of rice, as we know,
> Grows from his toil.

I did much better afterwards, for the daughter never coughed again. At the sight of the old man's buttocks raised high while he was digging, working so carefully—as if he were making a bed for an infant—my admiration for the people living in the countryside grew. It was extremely difficult to make a living here. Men's faces were rough, as wrinkled as walnuts—but their hands were strong. The women, by contrast, were fair-skinned and pretty. I wasn't there long before I saw that the locals truly treasured life. Their tenacity left a deep impression on me—so much so that I came to believe in the government's assertion that "city people need 're-education' in the vast countryside."

As city folk, we were told to mingle with the poor and lower-class peasants in the countryside. We depended on them for everything in the isolated area. We wakened very early during spring plowing, and it was still dark when we reached the area on the mount. About two hours later, someone would come with a very simple breakfast—just baked or steamed corn cakes with a bowl of millet soup.

There was no water for washing our hands, so we followed their custom of rubbing our hands with soil before we picked up the food, even though we'd just touched manure and excrement. Breakfast proceeded like this, and also lunch.

For the first few days in the village, I kept up my old habits, brushing my teeth and washing my face every day, but these habits proved a luxury. Our water supply was limited to a vat we kept inside our cave dwelling, which we filled up by carrying water from a well at the foot of the mountain, load by load. After a day's hard work in the fields, we had no strength left for that, so very soon my habits disappeared. So long as we had water for drinking and cooking, it was fine. Taking a bath or a shower was unheard of in the village. There were neither restrooms nor toilet paper. The locals wiped themselves with leaves in summer and earthen lumps in winter, simply rubbing a couple of times.

Doing laundry was another luxury. I expected my dirty clothes, repeatedly soaked in sweat, to stink. This was not the case. Even after a week or a month's use, my clothes smelled the same. The only difference was in the collars and cuffs, which gradually became more oily and shiny, just like those of the local peasants.

Of all the nuisances of country life, the worst was the fleas. So long as there were people or sheep kicking around, the fleas would never go hungry. Small as they were, these highly productive and elusive creatures, once having taken refuge in our clothing, refused to leave no matter what we tried. Because of the old sheepfold next to our cave dwelling, we had more fleas than anybody in the village. My bedding and a three-year-old blue cotton padded jacket became their paradise. My name happens to sound the same as "feeding sheep" in Chinese. The other youths often joked about this, at which all I could do was to give a wry smile. The fleas were very active at night—a simple bite by just one of them would leave that part of your skin swollen and itchy and have you scratching all night. After a while, I was able to sleep through the ceaseless torment. Exhaustion was something I was greatly thankful for. Once, in my dream, I became a flea, and I was very, very happy.

Hunger never really left us. The grain was far from enough, and meat or fat only appeared in dreams. I was forever hungry, like everybody else there. Even years later, my sister still remembered how I looked when I left after a home visit. When she and my mother saw me off at the railway station, she said, I was carrying a huge jute bag fully stuffed with food of different kinds. When I set out, hunched over by its weight, and looked back toward them to say goodbye, all they could see behind the bag was half of my dark and thin face, like that of a long-since malnourished refugee. Both she and Mother were heartbroken. Hunger was not just our "privilege;" the local peasants suffered from it, too. They toiled year in and year out, only able to grow barely enough food to keep themselves alive.

One day I made an important discovery about the local people. Of course they were hardworking, but each time they went out to labor in the fields, they were in low spirits.

Feng Huaicai, a man in his late forties, was our team leader. He was strong and healthy, and his complexion was reddish-black. The towel he wore on his head had long since lost its white color. He was kindhearted and sympathetic toward us. Every morning, he chanted a local tune to wake us up. Once, while we were hoeing a field, he suddenly told us to stop. "Take a break," he said. Confused, we asked him why we should take a break so early. "See," he said, his finger pointing toward the second team working across the gully, "they take so many breaks. Why should we work harder, when all of us are paid the same ten points a day? Let's loaf around on the job like they do."

His home was not far from ours. He had a son and a daughter. His daughter had married, while his son, though still a teenager, had proved to be a good farmer. He knew where and how to get good firewood. He taught us many farming tricks. Gradually, a friendship developed between me and his family. One day, Feng told me something I was fairly certain he hadn't confided in anyone else.

"We used to farm in our own fields," he said emotionally, "when we worked hard for a good harvest, and we had nothing to complain about in life. But after the communist method and the communes came, since 1957, things have gone from bad to worse. We don't even have enough food to feed the family." He said that he was unhappy with the production brigade accounting practices. "We're living on this hill," he explained, "and we have no idea what other people, on different hills, are doing. Still, at the end of the year, we have to share the harvest with them. In this situation, nobody wants to work hard. Men are paid ten points a day and women six, no matter how much difference you make at work." To drive his point home, he drew on a metaphor: "It's like a cooking pot with the same amount of rice in it. If the pot gets bigger, the porridge will be thinner and the portion for each person will be smaller."

These words made me think. I knew perfectly well that one of the crimes Liu Shaoqi and his successor Deng Xiaoping had committed was to promote the "three selves," meaning "more plots for private use; more free markets; and more enterprises with sole responsibility for their own profit or loss, fixing output quotas on a household basis." Mao had insisted on doing away with the practice.

Feng knew nothing about political struggle. He only spoke his mind, based on what he observed. I made similar observations and was equally confused. The issue would be addressed when China began to reform its policies after peasants from Xiaogang Village of Anhui Province risked their lives by secretly contracting farming production to each household. Their fields were managed equitably, for they rewarded every effort that anyone made. That autumn, a bumper harvest brought enough food for everyone in Xiaogang Village.

But this came much later. During the time when I was in Northern Shaanxi, the prevailing idea was to "have socialist weeds rather than capitalist rice seedlings." Feng and his fellow villagers were unable to make a change or do anything like those in Xiaogang Village.

As for me, I was tired of forever struggling against a ragingly empty belly, and my disappointment was fast turning into despair.

A REUNION

"AFTER BEING AWAY A LONG TIME," GOES AN AGE-OLD CHINESE saying, "you'll become nervous when you go back home." By 1970, I'd been working in the fields of Yan'an for a year. In the winter, when the fields were barren and the earth frozen solid, I set out to visit my parents for the New Year. It was my only holiday of the year and the only chance I had to see Father and Mother.

"Home" was no longer Beijing, but Henan Province, where my parents had been relocated for "re-education." They both worked in the fields there under the surveillance of local revolutionaries. It took months for my family's letters to reach me, and I had little sense of what was happening in their lives. How had my parents fared in the countryside? Had they been able to handle the heavy manual work in the fields? Did they have the strength to survive, or were their new lives breaking them?

The journey to Henan Province took many days. I set out

on foot, walking many miles before reaching a bus station
and then boarding a train. In my rucksack I carried a kilo
of salted pork I'd managed to buy on the black market
before leaving the Loess Plateau. For the whole length of the
journey, I imagined Mother's face when she'd unwrap the
package and see the pork. For the first time in years we'd
have dumplings with meat for the New Year. It was a small
gift, but just then it was all I had to give them.

✷✷✷

It was dusk when I finally reached my parents' village.
Following the locals' directions, I wandered along a muddy
road until I came upon a forlorn figure in the distance. Head
hanging low, the man was standing next to a dung pit about
twenty meters away from a tiny hut.

As I came closer I saw that the man was Father. My heart
sank at the realization.

"You're worthless!" a man was screaming at him.
"Totally, totally worthless!"

Father had always been particular with his appearance.
Back in Beijing, his clothes were simple but neatly pressed,
and he was always clean-shaven. He looked nothing like
that now. His hair was long and disheveled, and his skin had
turned coarsened and chafed. He was dressed in a cotton-
padded coat with a rope around his waist like a belt—
possibly for keeping warm.

But it wasn't so much his physical transformation that
frightened me, but the seeming change in his personality.
He'd always been such a stubborn person, but now he

seemed meek and obedient. He didn't utter a word as the man berated him, and that horrified me.

I quickened my step. "Father, I'm back!" I shouted out as I approached.

His whole body shuddered when he heard my voice. Sadly, the look of excitement on his face quickly disappeared. He flashed me a wink and said, "Go inside, your mother's in the house."

But I didn't do as he said. Instead, I turned to the man and asked, "What has my father done?"

Before the man could answer, Father quickly broke in with his own explanation. "I was pleading guilty to Chairman Mao for the mistake I committed today, and this man was helping me improve myself. Now, you go ahead and visit with your mother until we are finished."

I felt completely helpless. Fighting back angry, frustrated tears, I stepped into our "home," a strange place with bare walls and no furniture. In fact, until recently it had been a shed for animals. It looked a lot like the cave dwelling I had back in Yan'an. An icy blast swept over me, and I looked up. There was a large hole where the roof should have been. I watched a cloud pass swiftly past the dark sky. As a young man, I could handle this extreme discomfort, but how could my mother and younger sister bear it?

It was obvious from my first glance at her that Mother hadn't been bearing it well at all. Days spent shoveling frozen dirt into ditches had left their mark. She was thin and more fragile-looking than I had ever seen her. My sister Si Yan was smiling and pink-cheeked, but like Mother she wore two or three sweaters, long underwear, pants, and an overcoat inside the house to keep warm. Tears streamed down my face as Mother folded me into her arms.

Their circumstances were worse than I'd let myself imagine, especially Father's. Every morning before he went to work, he later told me, he reported to the production team's office for the Morning Ritual. In his case, this was not to ask instructions from Chairman Mao but confess the "mistakes" he'd committed the day before. After pleading guilty, he was reprimanded by someone from the production team. This went on nearly every day. He had to keep the *Little Red Book* with him at all times, even while working in the fields. On the day I arrived in the village, someone had informed on Father, claiming he'd mumbled Chairman Mao's words instead of reciting them loudly and clearly as he worked. Obviously he had an attitude problem and had to be punished.

We did have pork dumplings that year for the New Year Holiday. I made them myself, shaping the dough with my fingers and then tucking tiny portions of pork into the dough. I was still raging at the scene I'd witnessed earlier in the afternoon, but I tried not to show it. There was a fair amount of salted pork left over when I was done preparing the dumplings. After dinner I climbed through the big hole in the roof and carefully assembled the pieces onto some sticks. Once it was preserved, the pork would last a good while. At least they'll have some meat this year, I thought to myself as I climbed back down into the hut.

The next morning, I went outside to check on the meat only to find that every last piece was gone.

"It must have been the dogs," Father said, shaking his head sadly.

Even the dogs, I realized with a shudder, were starving in this barren, awful place.

✷✷✷

I returned to the Loess Plateau more dejected than when I'd left. Every morning, I woke at three o'clock to lead the donkey from its shed halfway up the hill to the bean curd mill at its shoulder. After maneuvering it in front of the mill, I put its blindfold on, and after that it began to turn the millstone. I placed tofu beans, which I'd soaked overnight, into the hole at the center, one spoonful after another. In this way, the beans were crushed, and after filtering the juice out, boiled in a huge iron pot until it concentrated into solid tofu.

I worked under surveillance alongside two counterrevolutionaries. One was the brigade veterinarian, whom I'd heard about but hadn't met, and the other, Old Lu. Old Lu's crime was that he'd worked as a low-level employee of the Kuomintang government before New China was founded—that was all. He had some schooling and was able to make tofu, so the brigade didn't give him a hard time. His talent for making tofu was not wasted.

Old Lu was talkative. Once, he proudly said to me, "I know about things down there in Beijing. You have tall buildings, meat to eat, and warm clothes to wear. Why did you young people come to this wretched mountain area and suffer?" Tears pricked my eyes. I could feel his sympathy, and I was touched.

Tofu was a luxury in the village, so its production was monitored down to the fine details: how many beans should be taken out from the brigade's warehouse, how much tofu should be made, and how much money it should fetch. Everything was carefully recorded in the accountant's book and verified on the spot.

During the first couple of days, my mouth watered at the steamy tofu and piping-hot soybean milk. How I wanted to take a bite, or just drink a little. Old Lu understood me. One day, he told me to take some when the soybean milk was boiling. It was quite a surprise. I cast him a doubtful look— did he really mean it, or was he just testing me? If I took it, the matter could become very delicate; it was a double-edged sword, for he could turn me in to gain favor from the village Party secretary, while I could report against him to the brigade. But the piping hot soybean milk smelled so good; its temptation was too much to resist. I took some. After the first mouthful, I put all my worries aside. Even if I was to be executed, I had to finish this wonderful delicacy first. How wonderful it was when the soybean milk came into my mouth, caressing my tongue, and kissing at my throat. Old Lu knew about my mixed feelings. To reassure me, he drank a little as well. I suddenly felt a sense of camaraderie, something I had long missed. Even if he were a "counterrevolutionary," I didn't care. My heart was warm.

Old Lu and I were charged not only with making tofu, but also selling it. This was a time when refrigerators were unknown and tofu could easily go bad. We had to get up very early and finish making it before 10 o'clock, at which time we began to sell it in the nearby town. The town was small, and the people living there were all working for the local government, post office, or grain supply center. They were paid by the government and received a grain ration.

Whenever we had a customer, I cut off a piece, weighed it, and took the payment. I felt like a merchant doing an honest business. Old Lu was very fair. He never pocketed a single coin. He would hand in the exact money to the brigade accountant. But I still had my doubts: Equality was the cornerstone in a socialist society, but why did these townspeople have money to buy tofu, while the villagers could not afford it?

We had another duty besides making and selling tofu—feeding pigs and breeding the ones the villagers kept. Inside the brigade's pigsty were baby pigs and a solitary boar. After we finished the tofu business in the morning, we fed pigs in the afternoon. Pig feed was not a problem with so much tofukasu around, and bran was always ready in the brigade's warehouse. Mixed with apricot leaves and wild herbs, it was perfect. After feeding, Old Lu and I were off to prepare pig feed for the next day. We would carefully lock the door before we set off up the mountain with a machete. Old Lu knew this place like the back of his hand. He knew where to find what we needed in different seasons. Spring was the season when the mountains exploded with wild herbs. It was a feast to the eyes.

Breeding pigs was a tough job. It was a time when the villagers owned nothing; they had no source of income beyond keeping a couple of sows. The piglets they bore were the source of cash for soybeans and lamp oil. The sows they kept were very thin from lack of food. These dirty creatures wandered about in the village, their teats hanging low from their bellies. Dirty as they were, their breeding cycle was fast and regular, with three fertile days every three weeks. Because of the huge demand, the breeding service was often fully booked. We had to keep them in line, for as soon as these sows smelled the boar inside, they became desperate, trying to get over the railing to be the first in. Our gentle efforts to keep them in line didn't work. We didn't want to hurt them. It was exhausting, but quite an amusing job. Their unconcealed desire relaxed our otherwise dull lives.

✵✵✵

I brushed shoulders with death twice on the Loess Plateau.

The cave I lived in was the highest in the village. With the frequent rains, the soil layer on its roof had gotten soaked through and the roof was loose and soft. One day, during a storm, it just caved in. Both Huang Meng and I were buried in soil. Lightning flashed and the thunder rumbled outside. How would anyone know what had happened and come to our rescue? Luckily, only the front part of the dwelling was buried, leaving a space toward the back free of soil.

Huang Meng and I dug desperately until we'd tunneled out into the rain. Every drop was a blessing from heaven, and I was so grateful to still be alive. It had been a close escape, and it taught me something: no matter how desperate the situation, just staying alive *was* a triumph.

The second time I faced death, however, I was strangely nonchalant about it.

One day I was out collecting firewood on the mountain. Firewood played an essential part in local life, as no electricity, gas, or coal was available. Cooking depended entirely on firewood. On the Loess Plateau, trees were few but bushes, many. The town of Zhengzhuang was close by, and residents had long since made use of the bushes.

On that day, while I was on duty collecting firewood, I had gathered a machete and some rope and traveled five miles to a gully. Huang Meng had heard there was plenty of wood in the gully. But when I got there I saw that all the bushes were up on cliffs, and to reach them, I had to hang myself from the top. Recently, someone in another county— also from Beijing—had fallen off a cliff and been killed while collecting firewood. At the news, we felt angry. But by that time, my view of death had changed. I was no longer scared at all. After collecting about ninety pounds of wood, enough for a full load, I was ready to go.

I made my way down on a very narrow mountain path. To my left was a cliff, and to my right, a deep gully. Was it dangerous? Yes, of course—but I didn't mind that, as every step I took had become mechanical. All at once a branch from a wild jujube plant hooked the firewood on my back. I lost my balance. My body was in the air. Fortunately, I managed to catch a branch and swing back onto my feet.

The feeling at that moment was so strange— indescribable, actually. Everybody treasures life, but at that moment, I wasn't scared. I felt *relief*. The reaction I'd had to catching the branch of that wild jujube to save my own life was pure instinct, nothing more.

I was about three miles away from home. The two corn pancakes I'd brought with me that morning were long gone. There was nothing left in my stomach. My legs were shaking. Several times, I tripped on something and fell to the ground. Once, I even wanted to lie like that on the ground forever. After stuffing a couple of handfuls of snow into my mouth to stave off my hunger, I got moving again. It was already midnight when I reached my cave, and I covered the last stretch of the path by crawling on all fours.

OUR LAND, BEAUTIFUL LAND

"PEOPLE WANT TO PLAY AN INSTRUMENT ON A FULL BELLY AND sing when their stomachs are empty." This is a common saying in China. I'd always loved to sing. Ever since I was a little boy, singing had been my favorite pastime. But I could never sing when I was hungry. Even if I tried, my pitch was always off when I sang on an empty stomach.

After I started working at the bean curd mill, this changed. I was less hungry, and my habit of singing came back.

Old Lu had a good voice. "Xin Tian You"—a sentimental old local folk song about life's sadness and happiness—was his favorite, and he could render it in a very impressive way. Its tune was simple but melodious, and almost everybody knew and could sing it. Whenever they were in the mood, the local people would stick out their necks and sing a little.

After a while I could sing some of these local folk songs, too. The first song I learned was "Lan Huahua," an old tune that everybody knew there:

Green threads, blue threads,
Green or blue, pleasing to the eye.
From them came a young girl named Lan Huahua,
A lovely girl everybody adores!

The lyrics were simple, but its tune was very melodious. Apart from local folk songs, Old Lu also knew some old songs from the Chinese south. Among them was *Picking Tea Leaves*:

A gentle breeze comes from the north,
In which we tea picking girls were busy in our garden.
We used to work for others,
Now, we work for ourselves.

My hometown in Guangdong Province had many tea gardens, and this song always made me homesick. Still, music consoled me in this desolate place. Each time we went up the mountain to collect wild herbs, we would sing something. The echoes in a ravine cheered us. Even the wild herbs seemed to be responding. I felt so good!

Remote as it was, this place also had ready ears for revolutionary songs from big cities. Once, while we were taking a break in a field, a peasant stood up, and after knocking his pipe against a stone to clear the ashes and coughing a couple of times to draw attention, he began a song entitled "Chairman Mao's Works Are Great!" Set to a folk melody, the song was very popular at the time:

People compare the sun to Chairman Mao's works,
To me, the sun is not up to them.
The sun rises and falls,
But Chairman Mao's works shine day and night!

The peasant was poised and very confident when he sang. People clearly took pleasure in his singing. Much to my surprise, as soon as he finished the song, a voice rose from the hill across the gully: "My sweetheart, I have missed you until my heart aches." It was from someone working in that area.

"Here comes a singing competition!" someone said.

He was right, for as soon as the man on the other side finished, a song rose from our side, followed by another from the other side, still another from our side, and still another from their side, until our team leader stood up and told us to stop singing and get back to work.

"Sweetheart, I have missed you until my heart aches!"

This line echoed in my ears all day long as I worked. The peasant who sang it was very courageous, I said to myself. Back in Beijing, he would have been arrested for "immoral behavior" for singing that love song.

That evening, while I was in bed, that line came back to bother me again. "I have missed you until my heart aches" kept resounding again and again. Yes, I had a girl etched deep in my heart. I had to admit it to myself. She was very pretty, like a blossom in the wilderness. Even as I buried my head in the quilt, I saw her in the darkness, in the depths of my heart.

She was a bright girl from an educated Beijing family. On the train coming from the capital, her voice had captured my attention. Melodious and sweet, each word she spoke was like a drop of water dancing in a mountain brook. Her face was round, her complexion fair, and her demeanor graceful. And her eyes weren't just pretty—they always seemed to be *saying* something.

One of the few books I'd brought from Beijing was a collection of folk songs from around the world, and "Santa Lucia," the famous Italian folk song, was my favorite. Its first line went: "Look, how bright the evening stars are!" Each time I sang this song, lying on a mountain slope carpeted by tender grass, the stars in the sky would transform into my sweetheart.

I was an avid reader, and from the stories I read, I had long since learned what love meant, but I had no idea at all what it felt like. Still, I was pretty sure that I liked this girl as more than just a friend. One day, when I heard she had brought some books on her recent trip home, I asked if I could borrow some. She agreed. Occasionally, when we worked together, I would steal a glance at her. Each time I felt reenergized. During a break from work, I would seek her out, dropping some casual excuse and chatting her up when no one was watching us.

Our first date—if it could be called a "date"—took place on a moonlit summer evening. I'd gone outside to fetch water at the foot of a hill. Her cave was close by and she happened to be standing outside it, looking up at the stars. A bright crescent moon hung low in the starry sky.

"Do you know any songs about bright stars in the evening sky?" she asked when she saw me approaching. "Or maybe a song about the moon?"

"Of course," I said, suddenly nervous. I cleared my voice and then began to sing "Santa Lucia":

> Sul mare luccica l'astro d'argento.
> Placida è l'onda, prospero è il vento.
> Sul mare luccica l'astro d'argento.
> Placida è l'onda, prospero è il vento.
> Venite all'agile barchetta mia,
> Santa Lucia! Santa Lucia!
> Venite all'agile barchetta mia. . .
>
> On the sea glitters the silver star.
> Gentle the waves, favorable the winds.
> On the sea glitters the silver star.
> Gentle the waves, favorable the winds.
> Come into my nimble little boat,
> Saint Lucy! Saint Lucy!
> Come into my nimble little boat. . .

The song had a beautiful melody and sweet words, and just then I felt I had Santa Lucia right beside me.

"Can you teach me to sing it?" she asked when I finished.

We sat down under a date tree in front of her cave dwelling and I started teaching her the words. These were perfect moments—pure and unsullied. When I walked back to my own cave dwelling afterwards, I was so happy I barely felt my feet touch the ground.

But that feeling couldn't last and it didn't. During the Cultural Revolution, love was a taboo, politically wrong, proof of a bourgeois mindset. Father and Mother were suffering in the countryside. Pursuing love under these circumstances would be selfish—not just disrespectful, but dangerous—so after that night I stifled my feelings, forcing them away.

★★★

Slowly and surely, I got used to life in this barren place, to the heavy labor day in and day out. Intellectuals and young students like me were regarded as lazy, incapable, and ignorant, unable to distinguish one crop from another. But I could do that and also much more. I had learned how to open up a wasteland, how to plow a field, how to sow seed, and how to make tofu. At the age of eighteen, I had good reason to call myself a fully qualified peasant.

But in my heart, I felt empty. My life was empty. How could I change my life? How could I make something of myself? It just wasn't within my power.

"Edison," Father said when I saw him at the next New Year holiday, "an American inventor with just three months schooling at primary school made 2,000 discoveries in his life. All the knowledge he had was self-taught."

"After a day's hard work in the fields," I said, "I'm exhausted and I don't have a shred of energy left to read."

At this Father said nothing, but he looked deeply pained.

I knew he was right, though. I had to pursue my studies, no matter how difficult my circumstances. Despite my hard-won skills, I wasn't really a peasant. I wasn't born in the countryside. All my life, Father had told me stories about his travels abroad. He'd shared his books with me. He and Mother had played us music from all over the world. And at my school in Beijing I'd had teachers from foreign lands; one of them, an Englishwoman, had once shown us slides of the Louvre, the Eiffel Tower, the Tower of London, the Rhine, sculptures from ancient Rome, and tribes people in Africa. I hadn't set foot outside China, but because of them—and my parents—foreign vistas had long since settled within me.

When I didn't have to struggle for food, these thoughts began to stir in me, but when I saw no way out, when I saw no hope of change, my heart sank.

Hope took an unexpected shape: a ping pong match. In a letter he wrote to me in the spring of 1971, Father told me about an upcoming visit by the American table-tennis team to Beijing, a visit organized by Zhou Enlai. I saw reports about the visit in my village's production brigade office. It seemed like something had changed, that the country might be opening itself up to the world. A strange feeling swelled in my chest, something absent so long I almost didn't recognize it: hope.

I had to pull myself together and study hard. I decided to begin with learning English. It was quite difficult when I had to start almost from scratch and had no teachers to help me. All I had was an English dictionary and *Voice of America*, which I listened to on Huang Meng's transistor radio.

Voice of America broadcast a regular English class for Chinese listeners, using *English 900*, a textbook from the Macmillan Company. It was quite a colloquial and practical textbook—just what I needed. Listening to *Voice of America* was a crime in those years, but my eagerness to study emboldened me. I was very thankful to Huang Meng, for he said nothing. How could he fail to notice my "strange behavior?" I'd stay up nights, listening to the radio in our cave while he slept. Sometimes, not wanting to disturb his sleep, I pulled my quilt over my head like a tent. To practice spoken English, I would say sentences aloud while I was alone in a gully.

But *Voice of America* was not always good to me. One night, listening to a news program inside my cave dwelling, I learned that NASA had sent a manned aircraft to the moon. The news was nothing less than a bomb, a bolt from the blue! The United States had long since carried out experiments, and its Apollo program had completed several successful flights. But now Neil Armstrong had left his footprints on the moon! "That's one small step for man, one giant leap for mankind," he'd said.

At this explosive news, a chill went down my spine. I felt something I had never felt before, something impossible to define. I turned off the radio and went outside. A bright moon was hanging low in the sky. At the sight of the moon, I usually thought about my family and felt homesick. But that evening, I was in a daze. The news of the moon landing was shocking. It had dislocated my old beliefs. *Those scientists are extraordinary,* I thought. *Compared to them I am nothing. I am no one.*

Suddenly, I lost interest in learning English. No matter how hard I studied, how many hours I devoted to the subject, a mere primary school student in an English-speaking country would have a better grasp of the language. What I should study, it suddenly dawned on me, was science, mathematics, physics, or chemistry. Didn't people say, "You have no worries at all after you study mathematics, physics, or chemistry?"

But where could I learn these subjects? Nobody was available to teach me, and I had no textbooks or resources of my own.

For years I'd felt guilty when I thought about my grandfather. During my last visit home, Father and I had sat on small stools outside. In the balmy sunshine of winter, he told me stories about Grandfather, how he had made his way through years of hard work, coming from a poor family, to becoming an overseas student in Japan. When he graduated, he returned to China, determined to do something to help his country.

The first thing Grandfather did was to make use of the knowledge he had picked up abroad by establishing modern accounting schools, one in Guangzhou and the other in Hong Kong. The second thing was to publish *English Grammar: Easy Parsing and Analysis with Chinese Translation* in 1909. He was the first in Chinese history to produce such a book. As soon as it was published, it was adopted into university curricula. Over the years it would be reprinted many times. Lin Yutang, a great Chinese scholar who was twice nominated for a Nobel Prize in Literature, lauded my grandfather as a "great linguist in China."

Even though my father didn't achieve as much as my grandfather did, he attended college and graduate school in the United States. He was fluent in many languages, and before the revolution felled him, he'd been a respected journalist.

It was now my turn to make something of myself, but how could I accomplish anything if I hadn't even finished high school? Sorrow and shame hooked into me and wouldn't let go.

But the campaign to relocate urban students to the countryside showed no signs of letting up. To take in more students from big cities, Inner Mongolia, Lanzhou, Yunnan, and Guangxi established their own production and construction corps. Even Tibet didn't allow itself to be left behind. I was convinced I would have to stay in this small village forever.

Once during this time, I managed to hear Beethoven's Symphony No. 5 in C Minor on the radio, a piece Mother used to play on the piano in Guangzhou. Years ago she had told me that Beethoven composed this piece after having lost his sense of hearing. She said he meant to encourage people to fight in an adverse situation, to be courageous enough to "cut fate by its throat."

When I felt especially despondent, I recalled this Beethoven symphony, humming it quietly to myself, but each time, I gave up after a few stanzas. I smiled bitterly. Not only did I lack the strength to cut fate's "throat," I didn't even know where that was anymore.

***

In the end, music altered my destiny.

Whenever I was in despair, music gave me strength and hope. This time it came in the form of an enchanting melody. The day after we harvested the millet, I passed Zhengzhuang Town on my way home. Just as I was about to enter a small shop to buy some kerosene oil for lighting, a tune drifted in the air and stopped me cold.

The melody was so beautiful that I forgot my mission, following the music instead. The road seemed suddenly bathed in sunshine. I eventually found myself inside the classroom of a local middle school at the western tip of the town. I had expected to see a pretty woman sitting before an organ; instead, it was a middle-aged man.

Even after he sensed somebody walking in, he didn't look back but continued playing. I stood there quietly listening.

After the piece was over, he turned around, giving me a gentle smile and said, "Oh, a young man from Beijing!" He was in his forties and bespectacled.

"You play very well," I said.

"Why not sing a song," he invited, "to accompany me?"

There was a song I learned at primary school, years ago. I was very familiar with it, so I began, letting out my voice in full:

> Our land, beautiful land,
> Jade green river water flows,
> Nourishing endless paddy fields
> Like undulating waves in the sea.

Lotus blossoms in quiet ponds,
Where golden carps, large and fleshy,
Are at happy play.

Ducks had made a home of the reeds,
The forest rustles in the wind,
Letting out a loud sound.

Lumbering workers are proud,
After they have felled huge trees
For building multistory buildings,
Factories and mines.

Behind the forest are mountains
Where deer and antelopes are frolicking.
Where people speculate
For mineral deposits.

High above in the sky are soaring eagles,
Guarding this land,
Now above grasslands, now above forests.

Music was truly magical. Instantly, the song shortened the distance between me and this stranger sitting before an organ. Following this encounter, we met often. His name was Li and he was a music teacher. I poured out my heart to him, telling him of my confusion and my regret at having given up my education. He offered to help by finding books I needed. He even volunteered to tutor me.

From then on, I had access to a variety of textbooks; from these I could cobble together a middle school curriculum. My hope was that someday I might manage to graduate from high school. Whenever I got confused, I went to Li for answers. He never failed me. His answers were always relayed with simple but precise words. He could explain even the most profound scientific questions. Because of Li, I happily lost myself in the pursuit of knowledge. My life became full and substantial. Most importantly, the pursuit of knowledge changed my fate.

★★★

One September day in 1971, I awoke to a fiercely blue sky. In the far distance, I could make out shreds of white above the mountains. Otherwise the sky was perfectly clear.

The day I left Zhengzhuang, my heart was light. I gathered up my few belongings and slung my rucksack over my back. As I walked toward the village, my head spinning, I was acutely conscious that I was alive and young on a beautiful day. One by one, the villagers came to meet me on the road. Men with white turbans and deep lines crisscrossing their sun-browned faces, girls with glossy black hair and bright red cheeks—they waved and called out well-wishes for my journey.

A truck had been sent to take me to Lintong. I clambered into the back, crouching under the tarp and looking out. Tomorrow I would report to my new work unit, Huaqing Hot Springs in Xi'an. This nearby tourist destination badly needed people who could speak foreign languages. They found my file and took me on as a tour guide.

It was my first salaried job, which was thrilling, but the best part of the new position was that it would vindicate Father. My accomplishment helped lift the taint of his so-called "counter revolutionary" past. Soon he and Mother would move out of their hut and into a decent home. Then, in the summer of 1971, Father was reassigned back to Beijing, where he would begin work as a typist. Mother soon followed him.

I will never forget the dazzle of the sunlight that day, or the soft autumn breeze that shook loose the gold leaves. When the truck rattled past the mountainside caves, I craned my neck and search for her, the girl I fancied. I didn't see her there. Suddenly, and very clearly, I knew that my feelings stemmed from immaturity—that and loneliness. Still, I wished I could have seen her one last time. While I didn't see her that day, I did see her cave. It was bathed in sunshine, warm and homey despite the bleakness surrounding it.

Outside the village, the road opened up to a broader vista and I looked out toward the Yellow River Valley. A reverent gasp escaped my lips. The river, with its massive banks of sediment, surged ahead into the distance. Trees and shrubs pressed against each side and the water shimmered wildly in the sun. Soon the floods would come, washing over last year's accumulation of windblown dust. The truck bumped and jerked along the road, but I paid no mind; in another hour I'd be crossing from the mud-packed road onto a major thoroughfare, north to Xi'an. This village had been my home, but I knew now that I didn't want to stay where I could not grow.

It was time to seek a place where I might make something of myself. It had taken many long years, but despite the obstacles, I was on my way at last.

AFTERWORD

TWO THOUSAND YEARS AGO, A THIRTEEN-YEAR-OLD KING BUILT a vast army to accompany him into the afterlife. In less than two decades, he would unify a collection of warring kingdoms and become China's first emperor. He standardized coins, weights, and measures; linked states with canals and roads; and built the first version of the Great Wall.

At thirteen, all that was still a long way off, but already he knew he would live forever. His only trouble was that he didn't wish to go into the afterlife alone.

Soon after he took the throne in 246 BC, the boy who became China's First Emperor began construction on his necropolis. Eventually, 700,000 laborers would produce some 8,000 life-sized soldiers, along with chariots and steeds, and when he died he took his place among them.

For many centuries, the First Emperor's mausoleum and vast terracotta army lay buried under the ground, hidden from earthly visitors. The region was riddled with underground springs and watercourses, and for centuries there had been reports of people finding pieces of old terracotta figures, tiles, bricks, and chunks of masonry.

In the 1970s, teams of archeologists were sent to investigate. Eventually, row upon row of massive clay statues would be unearthed in Xi'an, but I visited the site not long after the archeologists arrived to carve the first gigantic pit in the earth. I was young and self-conscious, and beside me stood a figure nearly as tall as one of the clay warriors, a man who'd change China's history and also my own.

✷✷✷

One month after I left Zhengzhuang, China's leadership faced a grim challenge: Lin Biao, Mao's comrade in arms, fled China for the Soviet Union. He never got there—he ran out of fuel and his plane crashed in the vast desert of Mongolia. Before his death, he had been the vice-chairman of the CCP Central Committee, and during the ninth CCP National Congress, he was made the successor to Mao. Overnight, he was declared a traitor—both against the Party and the country.

The world was left speechless, particularly the Chinese. It felt as if the whole nation had just been jostled out of a nightmare. Rubbing their eyes, they asked one another, "Why did this happen?" and "How did this happen?" Lin Biao's brutal end led many in China to feel disillusioned with the course of Mao's high-minded "revolution," which some people now felt had degenerated into a succession of power struggles, many of them led by Madame Mao and her cohorts.

If I had to trace the change in my own fate to one discrete source, it would be Dr. Henry Kissinger, President Nixon's National Security Advisor. To be precise, to the upset stomach Kissinger suffered on a state visit to Pakistan in

July 1971. To be even more precise, to the upset stomach he faked so that he could secretly fly to Beijing and meet Premier Zhou Enlai. That meeting would alter China's course—and also shape my family's future and my own.

In 1971, Father resumed his position as a translator and editor at *Beijing Review*. Although there were never any formal proceedings to overturn the political accusations against him, no more struggle sessions took place, and he was never again accused of spying.

Truly, China seemed on the verge of tremendous change.

Then, on July 16, came the explosive news: President Nixon would visit China before May 1972. On the day after the news was announced, the people's commune held a meeting for cadres in our village. At this meeting we heard more information about Nixon's upcoming visit. People were stunned. How was it, they asked one another, that the head of American imperialism had been invited to our country with so much fanfare?

I was secretly delighted. Recently, my father had written to tell me of a visit to China by the U.S. table-tennis team. It was a good beginning, Father said. A small window had been cut open in our walled-off world.

When I say Kissinger's secret visit to China changed my life, I don't mean it in just the symbolic sense. I'd been working as a tourist guide in Xi'an when I was assigned as one of the translators who accompanied Kissinger on his visit to the terracotta statues. Standing in the vast pit, encircled by the stately, long-hidden clay figures, I stood face-to-face with the first American diplomat to visit the country in more than four decades. I was so nervous that I don't think I did a very good job translating, but Kissinger was patient with me. He asked many questions about the statues and listened thoughtfully when I translated answers for him. His graciousness and inquisitiveness left a lasting impression on me, and the interaction fortified my hopes and ambitions.

More importantly, after Kissinger's visit to China, the country's heavy iron gate onto the outside world lumbered open. That trip paved the way for the groundbreaking 1972 summit between Richard Nixon, Zhou Enlai, and Chairman Mao Zedong, as well as the formalization of relations between the two countries, ending twenty-three years of diplomatic isolation and mutual hostility. In 1973, the Philadelphia Orchestra was invited to perform in Beijing and Shanghai, a landmark moment in China's history and a harbinger of cultural exchange with the West. People were now able to travel outside China's borders. This included me.

No official number has ever been put forth to establish how many people died during the Cultural Revolution. We will never know the true number of deaths. Millions of others suffered imprisonment, seizure of property, torture, or general humiliation. The Cultural Revolution's short-term effects may have been felt mainly in China's cities, particularly Beijing, but its long-term effects would impact the entire country for decades to come.

Long after the Cultural Revolution ended, I still felt very grateful to Mr. Li, the teacher I had met at the local school on the Loess Plateau. My thanks also went out to the Zhengzhuang villagers. Because of them, I was able to survive after a three-year exile on that isolated mountain. My time there changed me. First, I became strong. Whenever I later faced a challenge or hardship, I would remind myself that it was nothing compared with what I had gone through in Zhengzhuang. Second, I acquired knowledge. Back in Beijing, I'd had no choice but to leave school, but in the countryside I began to educate myself. Eventually I took wing when opportunity knocked, first to attend college in China, then to study in the United States, where I received my doctorate.

Fate—and my country's history—dealt me a bitter youth. If not immortality, I thought that by participating in the revolution I could grasp something beyond myself. Something great and lasting. All I caught was pain. But I'm grateful. Because of those bitter years, I became capable of understanding life, its hardships, and its gravity, and all kinds of strange twists of fate. Those years made me who I am. Fortunately, I didn't give up when I felt low. I fought to improve my circumstances, not only for myself, but for Father and Mother, who had given me everything and lost so much. I broke one barrier after another until eventually my life became vibrant and free.

A NOTE ON SOURCES

The following resources were useful in re-creating the events and period covered in this book.

Cheng Bi, *Nan Fang Zhou Mo Bao She,* February 7, 2014.

Du Zinan, "My Experiences at Peking University during the Cultural Revolution," *Hua Sheng Si Hai,* www.mhwh.com.

Feng Xuefeng, "Li Xuefeng: Mistakes of the First 50 Days of the Cultural Revolution—from the June 18 Incident to the July 29 Rally," *Zhong Gong Dang Shi Yan Jiu,* Issue 4, 1998 (CPC Party History Research Press).

Lin Yian, "One Night during the Cultural Revolution," *Nan Fang Zhou Mo Bao She,* March 23, 2011.

Luo Xiaohai, "The Ups and Downs of Red Guards: Notes from One at Tsinghua Middle School."

Mang Donghong, "How the Flame of Rebellion Was Ignited," *Dang Shi Bo Lan,* Issue 12, 2007 (Dang Shi Bo Lan Chu Ban She).

Ma Shengxiang, "Events of the Early Cultural Revolution at Peking University," *Wen Shi Jing Hua*, Issue 7, 2006 (Hebei People's Publishing House).

Yan Yangsheng, "The Cultural Revolution: the Birth, Violence and End of Red Guards," www.sina.com.cn (blog), January 22, 2014.

Yan Yangsheng, "One Hundred Days of the Red Guards from Tsinghua Middle School," *Yan Huang Chun Qiu* (Historical Happenings Retold), Issue 12, 2008.

Zhang Chengzhi, "The Era of Red Guards," Iwanami, Japan, 1992.

ACKNOWLEDGMENTS

I WOULD LIKE TO THANK THE SAN FRANCISCO BAY AREA independent bookstore Book Passage for its network of skilled publishing professionals, including Sam Barry, who leads the store's Pathway to Publication program. They provided essential resources and support during the writing of this book. Many thanks, too, to Barry Wootton and Sherry Wootton for first introducing me to Book Passage.

For creative support, my thanks to author Jasmin Darznik, a generous early reader who provided valuable insight that helped me shape a vivid story from my long-ago memories. Thanks also to the creative talents of Jim Shubin, whose graphic design lends *Red Fire* its visual power.

I am also indebted to the many friends and former school-mates who lived through the Cultural Revolution with me. They include Li Guoqing, Liu Wuning and Yu Yuan, who helped me sharpen my recollection of events that took place a half century ago.

A special note of thanks goes to Guo Bingyi for giving me a great deal of assistance in writing the Chinese manuscript. My sister, Zhao Siyan, helped me assemble the family photos and historical records necessary to compose this account. I also greatly appreciate my business colleagues in Beijing,

Catherine Li and Mei Dong, for their assistance on this project.

My deepest thanks go to my late parents, Bingquan Zhao and Jie Qin, who taught me to be a caring person and who shared their love of Chinese history and culture with me.

Finally, to my supportive wife, Ping, I offer great gratitude. She was the one who first encouraged me to write this memoir. She, together with my other family members, Sharon Chao Wootton, Jeff Wootton, Angela Chao, and Bryan Chao, offered invaluable encouragement from beginning to end.

ABOUT THE AUTHOR

Wei Yang Chao was born in Guangzhou in southeastern China and moved with his family to Beijing in 1965, on the eve of the Cultural Revolution. In the aftermath he worked as a translator and tour guide, speaking Mandarin, Cantonese and English. In 1981 he came to America to study at the University of California, Berkeley, where he received both his Master's and Ph.D. degrees. He later obtained engineering training at the Massachusetts Institute of Technology. Pursuing a career in innovative business technology, he founded one of China's "Top 100" e-Business and Internet companies and served as Chairman/CEO for sixteen years.

He now lives in both the San Francisco Bay Area and Beijing, working to promote cultural understanding and exchange between China and the United States. He is the author of many books and articles in Chinese on the topics of technology and culture. *Red Fire* is his first major publication in English.

Made in the USA
San Bernardino, CA
15 August 2017